7th HEAVEN

7th HEAVEN

CELEBRATING SHABBAT WITH REBBE NACHMAN OF BRESLOV

MOSHE MYKOFF

WITH THE BRESLOV RESEARCH INSTITUTE

JEWISH LIGHTS Publishing

Woodstock, Vermont

7th Heaven:
Celebrating Shabbat with Rebbe Nachman of Breslov

2003 First Jewish Lights Quality Paperback Edition
© 2003 by the Breslov Research Institute

Original hardcover edition published by the Breslov Research Institute, Jerusalem/New York.

Library of Congress Cataloging-in-Publication Data
Mykoff, Moshe.
7th heaven : celebrating Shabbat with Rebbe Nachman of Breslov / Moshe Mykoff.
  p. cm.
ISBN 1-58023-175-6 (pbk.)
1. Sabbath (Jewish law) 2. Prohibited work (Jewish law) 3. Bratslav Hasidim. 4. Hasidism. I. Title: Seventh heaven. II. Title.
BM685 .M95 2002
296.4'1—dc21

                                                                2002153421

10 9 8 7 6 5 4 3 2 1

Manufactured in Canada

Published by Jewish Lights Publishing
A Division of LongHill Partners, Inc.
Sunset Farm Offices, Route 4, P.O. Box 237
Woodstock, VT 05091
Tel: (802) 457-4000   Fax: (802) 457-4004
www.jewishlights.com

Rebbe Nachman Taught:

It's not enough for us to experience Shabbat only once a week. We should try to experience the otherworldly delight and joy of Shabbat on the weekdays as well. Anyone who looks to tomorrow for his reward from God has not fully worshiped Him today.

(Likutey Moharan I, 5:2)

CONTENTS

3 | ג

SHABBAT: THE MORNING

4 | ד

SHABBAT: THE AFTERNOON

5 | ה

SHABBAT: ON THE WAY OUT

Acknowledgments

In the laborious birthing of this work, many have lent encouragement and advice, though none more than the one who conceived it—Chaim Kramer.

I am grateful to Jay Knopf, whose generous support enabled the book to see the light of day.

Many thanks to the following people whose voices have entered the book in some way, large or small: Yitzchak Attias, Akiva Atwood, Ozer Bergman, Dave Greenfield, Abba Richman, Esther Rubenstein, and Eliezer Shore. To Shaul Magid—where the mind sees two, the heart sees one and is inspired.

My deep thanks to Sara Chava Mizrahi, whose magisterial editing gave the book style and correctness. In this work, as in the others on which we have collaborated, she perseveringly prodded me to write the best that I could.

My greatest debt in writing this book is to my wife, Elky, for the love and patience that made it possible and the incisive suggestions that made it immeasurably better.

I offer this work in loving memory of my parents, R' YISROEL and RIVKAH MYKOFF, and my parents-in-law, R' SHEYA LEIB and SOSI HALPERT—four who knew well the meaning of personal sacrifice in their faithful observance of the Shabbat.

MOSHE MYKOFF
Jerusalem

Introduction

SHABBAT has never been so popular.

People from all walks of life are discovering the wonderful benefits of setting aside one day a week to "unplug"—no phone, no stereo, no computer—letting go of all unfinished business, leaving the week's work and worries behind. The benefits of turning down the volume of the outside world, even just once in seven days, are irrefutable. Whether it is to reconnect with family and friends, to pause our overscheduled itineraries to focus on the wonder and beauty of life, or to recharge ourselves physically and spiritually—Shabbat shows us the way.

Yet there is a more fundamental and a far more fascinating dimension of Shabbat that warrants our attention. It is the dimension that relates to the inherent holiness God intended for that day when He sanctified it at Creation, the spiritual energy that leads us to the wholeness and harmony that only the seventh day can generate. Here we discover the soul of the Jewish Shabbat.

The day of rest that has attained media limelight may point us in the right direction, yet its best-selling benefits are not so very different ultimately from those we might derive from a meditative Monday or a relaxing Wednesday. The fashionable adaptation of Shabbat that so many books and articles portray is unlikely to help us capture the greater part of the day's singular spirit and consciousness.

The key to unlocking the most vital dimension of Shabbat is mitzvah.

Most of us know mitzvahs as "commandments," as the laws and customs that comprise the dos and don'ts of Jewish life. But this understanding barely scratches the surface of what the mitzvahs are. The Hebrew word *mitzvah* connotes "togetherness" and "connection." When someone performs a mitzvah, he or she is creating a unique bond with God; the ritual laws and customs are the means by which we can come close to God and experience His presence.

Mitzvahs bind the personal with the supernal; they are deeds that involve thought, word and physical action and are thus the channels through which we draw God's Infinite Light into our finite universe and limited human consciousness. Each mitzvah we perform, every action that is in alignment with God's Will, is yet another opportunity for primary contact with the spiritual energy and the consciousness that nourish our soul-life.

On the deepest of levels, the mitzvahs embody ancient secrets, passed down through the ages by our tradition, for refining our spiritual insight, for aligning the microelements of the personal universes of man with the macro-elements of the cosmos. Mitzvah is among the most effective means in our spiritual repertoire for gaining entry to the inner spiritual framework inherent in all of Creation. It is also a means of establishing a dialogue between ourselves and the cosmic reality. The energy invested in the physical acts we perform activates parallel spiritual energies in the supernal realm; each act and every prayer becomes a conduit connecting us to God, as well as a channel for God's influence and blessing to descend into the world and into man.

At no time is this truer than on Shabbat, when the day's special mitzvahs are our most direct means for linking the world's micro- and macro-dimensions. Through the disciplines of practice and prayer we find the path to experiencing sanctity and harmony in our lives. Whether fashioned of custom or of halakhic requirement, the Shabbat mitzvahs form the gateway through which we make contact with the higher consciousness and holiness exclusive to the seventh day.

Although Shabbat is set in time, fixed in the cosmic tapestry, and so essentially unaffected by human actions, man nevertheless has an essential role to play in the day's elements unfolding each week. The sanctity and higher consciousness of the seventh day are channeled into the world primarily through human agency.

By observing the Shabbat we become God's collaborators in Creation. When we rest on the seventh day and give rest to the world around us, just as God did on that first Shabbat, we increase the tranquility and harmony in the universe. Being mindful of the day and relating to it through concrete actions grounded in mitzvah, we infuse our personal universes with holiness and wholeness. To the degree that we sanctify the Shabbat day, through the quality of our God-consciousness and rest, we directly influence the flow of Divine blessing to Creation.

To enhance our performance of the mitzvahs of Shabbat, we need to deepen our understanding of their meaning and purpose. Deeper understanding leads us to greater intentionality (*kavanah*), to actions consciously performed. The more we focus on the *why* of the *what* and *how* of our Shabbat observance, the more complete will be our experience of Shabbat, both on the cosmic and on the personal levels.

This book is meant to bring that greater meaning and mindfulness to our Shabbat observance. Each of its essays offers a deeper look at one of the laws, customs or prayers that together form the body of the mitzvahs of Shabbat.

There are numerous English-language books (and Internet sites) that explain the laws and lore of the week's holiest day; those first learning to walk the walk of Shabbat would do well to avail themselves of the excellent introductory material these works provide. Few, however, are the works that address the art of keeping Shabbat consciously, and fewer still are those that explore the nature of the different time frames of the seventh day or the place of each mitzvah within the greater Divine design. This book presents to the English-reading public the deeper meaning and purpose of a broad range of Shabbat observances. It attempts to provide an in-depth under-standing of the day's traditional religious practices within the context of life's spiritual micro-macro dynamics, and seeks to give a sense of how the day's mitzvahs fit within the comprehensive scheme of the elaborate Shabbat mosaic.

The essays presented herein are based on the insights and teachings of Rebbe Nachman of Breslov (1772–1810) and those of his foremost disciple, Reb Noson (1780–1844). While their teachings have been restated here in contemporary language and within the context of modern times, the deep insights into Torah and spirituality revealed by these great Chassidic luminaries are as relevant in today's world as they were some two centuries ago, when they were first taught.

The first to paint a "Breslov portrait" of Shabbat was Reb Nachman of Tcherin (d. 1894), a leading figure of third-generation Breslov Chassidism. His technique of isolating those sections of Rebbe Nachman's lessons and Reb Noson's discourses that speak of the seventh day's mitzvahs formed the basis of the approach you will discover in these pages.

Each of the essays in this book can stand alone, and so the book need not be read straight through; the reader can open to the particular Shabbat mitzvah he or she wishes to explore. Nevertheless, reading consecutively will afford a better understanding of where a given mitzvah fits into the broader picture of Shabbat. An excerpt from a primary halakhic source outlining a Jewish law or custom introduces each teaching, providing a bit of background for each specific practice. Some of the essays are accompanied by short inspirational messages of Rebbe Nachman, based on a theme mentioned in the essay; the mindfulness we seek on Shabbat is sometimes best sparked through inspiration of the heart.

This book is divided into five sections, each of which examines one of the five time frames of Shabbat. The predominant theme of the first section, "Shabbat: On the Way In," is that of letting go of the week and preparing to celebrate Shabbat. The majority of the mitzvahs that form "Shabbat: The Night," the second section, relate to the ascent into holiness and the contemplative atmosphere that comes with the onset of Shabbat. The practices that make up "Shabbat: The Morning," the third section, focus primarily on expanding awareness. The fourth section, "Shabbat: The Afternoon," highlights the parallel between the cosmic oneness at the climax of the holy day and the wholeness and harmony that can be ours through Shabbat observance. The essays of "Shabbat: On the Way Out," the fifth and final section, relate mostly to carrying Shabbat holiness over to the week, drawing the higher consciousness of the seventh day into the "everyday" of our lives.

If keeping Shabbat is new to you, or if you've experienced it only in its popular form but would like to deepen your understanding and connection through mitzvah—this book is for you.

If keeping Shabbat is something you grew up with, but you were never taught the deeper meaning of all the mitzvahs and customs you were told to obey, or if you were never shown how Shabbat observance could guide you to personal and spiritual growth—this book is for you.

If keeping Shabbat has never been a part of your spiritual practice, but you would like to learn more about the Jewish pathway to wholeness and higher consciousness through the only ritual observance mentioned in the Ten Commandments—this book is for you.

We experience the spirit of Shabbat as an inward event, one that quickens both heart and soul. But it is good to remember that Shabbat exists beyond us as well, touching our mountains and streams and cities, affecting, too, worlds higher and more spiritual than our own. On Shabbat, without exception, every corner of creation is uplifted by an extra measure of spiritual energy.

When the seventh day arrives we look at the world with eyes of a higher reality. Shabbat offers us a vision of the world not as it is but as it has the potential to be; indeed, as it one day will be—in the World to Come. God gave us the mitzvahs of Shabbat so that we might tap into the day's spiritual dimension. He gave us these mitzvahs that we might experience the great delight that observing

Shabbat affords; a delight that prompted our Sages to call the seventh day "a preview of the World to Come"—a taste of "7th HEAVEN."

A NOTE TO THE READER:

The essays in this book draw on Rebbe Nachman's lessons in *Likutey Moharan* and Reb Noson's discourses in *Likutey Halakhot*, as well as Reb Nachman of Tcherin's *Yekara DeShabbata* and *Nachat HaShulchan*, two works that proved indispensable for decoding the esoteric Kabbalistic teachings that are the basis for many of the Shabbat mitzvahs. The sources for the essays can be found in a separate section at the end of the book.

Hebrew terms are explained the first time they appear in an essay; the reader can also find these words in the glossary at the end.

Although the Holy One will sometimes manifest through typically masculine or feminine attributes (we speak of the "masculine face" or "feminine face" of the Divine), God is neither male nor female but entirely beyond the . dualistic distinctions of gender. English, however, has yet to formulate a gender-neutral pronoun, and so attempting to reflect God's gender-inclusiveness in the text would have proven stylistically awkward. Thus, while recognizing the sensitive nature of this issue, I've elected to retain the traditional forms of reference to God, "He" and "Him." I've likewise followed the traditional style in occasionally using the word "man" as a generic term referring to all human beings.

1 | א

SHABBAT:
ON THE
WAY IN

On the Way In:

Introduction

"I have a precious gift in My treasure vault,"
God told Moshe.
"Its name is Shabbat.
I intend to give this gift to the Jewish people.
Go inform them."

(Shabbat 10b)

*E*xperiencing Shabbat takes preparation. God let us know in advance about this precious gift, that we might gear up for it. To jump from a stationary position into the upward movement of holiness of any kind is all but impossible, and this is certainly the case when it comes to the unique holiness of Shabbat. The preparations we make in honor of the seventh day give us the running start we need.

Preparing for Shabbat means many things. It begins with our looking forward to the upcoming Shabbat and anticipating its arrival from the moment Shabbat ends. This is the meaning of the Torah's instruction, "Remember the Shabbat" (Exodus 20:8). From the very first day—even the very first moment—of the week, we are to remember it. The first-century Talmudic sage Shammai did just that.

A person should rise early on Friday morning in order to prepare all that is necessary for Shabbat. Even if one has a full staff in one's employ, one should make it one's business to prepare something personally in honor of the holy day. Thus Rabbi Chisda would mince the vegetables; Rabbah and Rabbi Yosef would chop wood; Rabbi Zeira would light the fire; Rabbi Nachman would arrange his house, bringing out those items needed for Shabbat and clearing away objects used only during the weekdays.

We should all follow the example of these sages and not say, "Don't expect me to belittle myself [with such menial activities]!" On the contrary, it lends one dignity to honor the Shabbat by preparing for its arrival (Shulchan Arukh, Orach Chaim 250:1).

Whenever Shammai ate, he kept Shabbat in mind. On any weekday, if he acquired some tasty food he would set it aside for Shabbat; if something even more desirable then came his way, Shammai would eat the other food and set aside the better one for Shabbat.

The bulk of our Shabbat preparations are reserved for Friday. The mitzvahs we perform to get ready for Shabbat, both the halakhic requirements and the customs, fall into two parallel categories: outer cleansing and inner cleansing.

In a general sense, outer cleansing relates to preparing our homes and our bodies; it includes purchasing, preparing and sampling the foods to be served at our Shabbat meals, readying the Shabbat table and donning fine garments in honor of the holy day.

Inner cleansing relates to preparing our minds and our hearts, shedding the negative feelings and qualities that have clung to them through our involvement in the marketplace. These preparations include reviewing the weekly Torah portion, immersing in a mikvah, and sitting in secluded meditation and self-evaluation, examining all our actions, words and thoughts of the week gone by.

Then, as sundown approaches, we detach ourselves from all weekday involvements and refrain from the "work"—the creative activity (*melakhah*)—that the Torah proscribes on Shabbat. Reciting the special prayers and psalms of Friday afternoon gives us the strength to let go of the week; we begin to enter the Shabbat state of mind, leaving our weekday worries and trials behind us.

In a more general sense, preparing for Shabbat is representative of man's purpose in the world. The weekdays are to Shabbat what this world is to the World to Come—both the weekdays and our existence in the world are preparatory stages for something far greater.

The Talmud sets forth the principle: Only one who has prepared beforehand will be able to eat on Shabbat. This is true on the spiritual plane as it is on the physical. We cannot expect to enjoy all the wonderful spiritual delights of Shabbat—the inner calm, the higher awareness, the sense of connection and oneness—unless we have prepared ourselves during the week. All our spiritual devotions in this world are the preparations we make to enable us to receive the precious gift that God wants us to have: *the gift of Shabbat.*

Charity
and Expenses:
Spiritual
Currency

A person with means is required
to honor the Shabbat
commensurate with his ability...
[but] if one has nothing and
must rely entirely on charity,
the charity trustees are obligated
to give that person at least
three meals and some treats.

(Mishnah Berurah 242:1)

One should limit one's weekday expenditures
in order to save money to honor the Shabbat.
Let no one say,
"How am I ever going to save anything?"
On the contrary,
the more one spends for Shabbat,
the more one will have.

(Tur, Orach Chaim 242)

*T*he soul wants nothing more than to grow in its own ways, journeying ever closer to the Source of its spiritual sustenance. Shabbat is a weekly catapult for the soul; it can propel us in the direction the soul wants and needs to go. Yet for Shabbat to aid us most effectively, we have to prepare ourselves for the journey. Making the most of the forward thrust that Shabbat offers requires our cultivating qualities and attitudes that make our hearts more spiritually sensitive.

During the week there are numerous forces at work in this world that would deny us the vitality of Shabbat and undermine our spiritual progress. These forces affect the places deep within us, places in which we are ethically and spiritually most vulnerable. If they prevail, these adversaries can render us indifferent and spiritually numb, and in doing so can keep us from the vitality and consciousness the soul desires.

Our attitude toward money is one aspect of our consciousness that is particularly vulnerable and so especially beleaguered. When we are caught in a rut worrying about whether we have enough money; when we are despondent over the fact that we don't have enough; when we invest all our energy and thought into earning more of it—then the troublesome forces of negativity have scored a victory.

Even so, what would we do without money? Money is one of life's necessities; we have no choice but to involve ourselves in the pursuit of a livelihood.

Beyond ensuring personal financial security, conducting our business practices honestly and with faith in God is essential for *tikkun olam*—the world's social and spiritual transformation into what God meant it to be. Effecting this transformation is our responsibility as human beings; therefore on some level we *must* engage the circumstances that lure us to the pursuit of money. And yet it is precisely this compelling appeal of money that opens the way to the forces that would undermine our spiritual development.

Preparing for Shabbat provides us with two magnificent opportunities to overcome the spiritual insensitivity that is spawned of the adverse allure of money. The first is to give charity to those who don't have enough money to purchase their Shabbat needs or, in the same vein, to host them at our Shabbat tables. The second is to use the money we've earned to honor Shabbat by purchasing and preparing the tastiest food, the best drink and the finest clothing we can afford.

Both of these remedies—sharing our resources with others and investing our money in the special Shabbat expenditures—raise the level of our heart's spiritual sensitivity. By allowing spiritual values to determine our expenditures we loosen money's hold on us and ease our attachment to it. The freedom that then becomes ours propels us forward along the spiritual odyssey that is Shabbat. 🕎

REVIEWING THE TORAH PORTION:
TRANSLATING SECULAR INTO SPIRITUAL

Every week, one should read over
the weekly Torah portion
[read in synagogue on Shabbat],
twice in Hebrew and once in *Targum*,
Aramaic translation.

(SHULCHAN ARUKH, ORACH CHAIM 285:1)

One who does not understand the Aramaic
may read, as *"Targum,"* a translation of the portion
rendered into one's mother tongue,
provided the translation includes commentary
based on the teachings of the Sages.

(MISHNAH BERURAH, IBID.:5)

The ideal time for this is Friday morning,
as part of one's Shabbat preparations.

(MINHAGEI HAARI, INYANEI SHABBAT 9)

*J*ewish teaching traditionally identifies three distinct facets of the human consciousness: wisdom-*chokhmah*, understanding-*binah*, and knowledge-*daat*.

Chokhmah, wisdom, is human thought manifest as profound revelation, as the proverbial flash of light that leaves us feeling intense wonder and awe (see insert).

CHOKHMAH is all the axiomatic principles that define existence. From the basic rules of nature to the rudimentary concepts of mathematics to the fundamental elements of cognition that underlie all our thought processes—these all fall under the general rubric known as *chokhmah*-wisdom.

BINAH is the expansion and interplay of axiomatic principles, from which emerge a logical structure or a coherent system of laws. In the field of mathematics, for example, if we take the ten digits from zero to nine and, applying various principles, process them through our faculty of understanding, we can obtain the entire corpus of mathematics (Innerspace, p. 59).

In the realm of human consciousness, *chokhmah* is pure, "undifferentiated mind"—the calm clarity of a non-dualistic mind that perceives everything at the level of its essence, and in doing so causes us to experience a deep sense of connection to all things.

Binah, understanding, is the intellectual processing of wisdom. It is the womb in which wisdom gestates, the seedbed that nurtures the flash of *chokhmah* and enables it to blossom by degrees into a complex organism of thought (see insert).

In the realm of human consciousness, *binah* is "discerning mind"—the intuitive perception of a differentiating mind that perceives everything from a position of objectivity born of separation and distance from it.

Daat, knowledge, the third facet of the human consciousness, is the synthesis of *chokhmah*, wisdom, and *binah*, understanding. We might think of this confluence of undifferentiated mind and discerning mind as balanced thought.

In the realm of human consciousness, *daat* is "integrative mind"—the ability to bring together the axiomatic information (wisdom) and follow it to its logical extension (understanding). Whereas *chokhmah-* and *binah-*consciousness are the internal workings of the intellect, *daat-*consciousness is its externalizing force; it is logic in its applied form. Daat is also the ability to express one's intelligence to others, to communicate one's inner thoughts effectively.

As the vehicle for deep and intense communication, *daat-*consciousness indicates the efficacious use of language. This essential function is reflected in the concept of *Targum*, the translation of Torah. For the Torah to be communicated to the people effectively, the original Hebrew had to be rendered into Aramaic, the language spoken by the majority of Jews in Talmudic times.

Targum, like *daat-*consciousness, more broadly signifies the externalizing of intellect, for it is the translation of wisdom and understanding—the internal workings—into everyday expression.

We live our lives absorbed in the business of *Targum*, in the struggle to communicate effectively, both to others and to ourselves—especially to ourselves—the wisdom and understanding inherent in human existence. We are engaged constantly in the challenge of application, of translating the axiom-like ideals and structures of the Torah and of life in general into the less-than-ideal realities of this world. Coping with the many contradictions of life, integrating what should be and what is, comes only with *daat*-consciousness.

Shabbat consciousness, too, comes only with the integration of *chokhmah* and *binah* through *daat*-consciousness. Just as the body requires spiritual cleansing to enable us to experience the extra measure of holiness that imbues all corporeality on Shabbat, so does the mind require spiritual preparation to enable us to experience the extra measure of consciousness that suffuses the entire world on the seventh day.

On Friday we read the weekly Torah portion twice in Hebrew and then a third time in Aramaic. The first Hebrew reading corresponds to *chokhmah* and the second to *binah*, and the third reading in translation corresponds to *daat*. The words of the Torah in Hebrew, the language of profound revelation and coherent structure, prepare us for our experiencing of Shabbat consciousness. In ways that only the soul can sense, reading the weekly portion in Hebrew introduces us to an awareness of undifferentiated mind that connects with the essence of everything in creation, and to an awareness of discerning mind that begets insight and intuitive perception.

Yet without reading the Torah portion a third time in the Aramaic translation, our preparation remains incomplete. While the Hebrew speaks to the innermost aspects of the mind, it does not communicate with the outer aspects— with those elements whose daily involvement in this world causes them to come up against the less-than-ideal realities of life. Only with *daat*-consciousness, the *Targum* of Torah, comes the power to free the mind completely of its weekday consciousness and concerns. Only with the awareness of integrative mind are we able to redirect our thoughts from the worldly and the secular to the spiritual and the Divine.

With the balanced consciousness that we gain through integrating the Hebrew words of the Torah with the *Targum*, our reading the Torah's weekly portion on Friday sets in motion the *tikkun* that has been ours to fulfill ever since the first human was created on the first Friday of Creation: instilling our minds—and through our minds, everything in God's world—with the higher consciousness of Shabbat. שבת

Trimming
the Nails:
Manicuring
a More Perfect
Existence

It is a mitzvah
to clip one's nails on Friday,
in honor of Shabbat.

(Shulchan Arukh, Orach Chaim 260:1)

When God banished Adam and Eve from the Garden of Eden for eating from the Tree of Knowledge of Good and Evil, He took from them the garments of pure light in which their souls had been clad. God then clothed their souls in a layer of skin whose sheen, a faint afterglow of its original radiance, resembled the luster of human nails. The corporeality of their new garments bore testimony to the body's inevitable demise; humanity's opportunity for immortality in this world was lost.

The Kabbalists explain that exchanging Adam and Eve's original garments with a nail-like covering of skin was a message from God: By ingesting the forbidden fruit, these representatives of humanity had ingested evil and made it an intrinsic part of their being. They had turned mankind's challenge to sort out good from evil into an *internal* struggle. Whereas prior to that time this struggle touched their lives only insofar as they encountered evil outside of themselves, thereafter, the major battlegrounds on which this war would be waged would be the body, the heart and the mind.

Once good and evil became inexorably intermingled within man, his very essence became filled with contradiction. Truth—originally apparent and unqualified—became clouded and incomplete. Distinctions between right and wrong, between the pure and the impure—initially absolute and evident—became relative and mired in ambiguity. Evil—formerly personified in the external manifestation of the snake—became mankind's internal voice of impulse and physical desire. The obscuring of the pure light attested to the dimming of God-consciousness that was caused by the sin of the first humans; God's presence could no longer be detected in the world without first overcoming daunting obstacles. The nail-like garments of the first humans signified the obscurity of this internalized struggle between good and evil.

Nowadays our bodies are even more corporeal than were Adam and Eve's. Our minds and hearts, too, struggle to recover clarity and consciousness long lost. The nails of our fingers and toes—the last vestiges of their nail-like garments—testify to a further loss, that of a vivacity and life spirit no longer ours. Being dead matter, the nails symbolize our lifelessness—those parts of our personalities that have stopped growing spiritually. This is especially true of the ends of the nails, which, since they extend beyond the fingertips, are extraneous to the body and contribute nothing to its functioning.

Unless removed, the dead elements in our lives—a relationship that is no longer healthy, a behavior that has ceased to empower us—drain our energy and life spirit and arrest our spiritual growth.

Shabbat is the spark that jumpstarts our spiritual growth and rejuvenates the life spirit. Shabbat is our enduring link to the eternal world, to the world Adam and Eve inhabited before God banished them from the Garden. On Shabbat we can step back from our involvements in the realm of the material and the mundane to focus on life's spiritual side. The tranquility born of freedom from the tyranny of life's daily demands quells our inner contradictions.

In the calm that is Shabbat, truth becomes more apparent, right-from-wrong more obvious, the obstacles to detecting God's presence less daunting. Shabbat is a chance—if but for a night and a day—to sense what life was like before our souls lost their garments of light.

To help ready ourselves for this experience we trim our nails. Removing the lifeless matter from our bodies effects a separation of evil from good, eliminating this remembrance of our mortality that arose from Adam and Eve's eating from the Tree of Knowledge. The act of trimming our nails, therefore, serves as a limited rectification of their sin. Clearing away a portion of the lifeless negativity that surrounds our week enables us to rediscover in Shabbat the spark and the vitality of a more perfect existence. ◉

SHABBAT JOY

Take note of the heaviness that accompanies the weekday mitzvahs; it is a mark of the lifeless, uninspired way in which we perform so many of our good deeds and devotions.

Dispel the weekday-heaviness by preparing for Shabbat. Suffuse your preparations with the extraordinary joy of Shabbat. Then the pathways to God will open wide to receive your mitzvahs—even those mitzvahs that are far from perfect, those made heavy by the absence of your own heartfelt involvement, will lift you up to God.

(Likutey Moharan I, 277; II, 2:5)

BATHING
AND IMMERSING
IN A MIKVAH:
THROUGH FIRE
AND WATER

To prepare for Shabbat,
it is a mitzvah to bathe one's entire body,
or at the very least one's face, hands and feet,
in hot water.

(SHULCHAN ARUKH, ORACH CHAIM 260:1)

After reading over the weekly Torah portion
twice in Hebrew and once in Aramaic translation,
Rabbi Yitzchak Luria (the preeminent 16th century
Kabbalist of Safed known as the holy Ari)
would immerse in a mikvah.

(MINHAGEI HAARI, INYANEI SHABBAT 9)

*T*he soul and the body are partners in this life, joined within the dynamic being we call a human. Theirs is a shared venture, at the end of which they are separated temporarily, only to be reunited thereafter for all eternity.

The body is the soul's outer garment, the means by which spirit interfaces with the physical world. Yet the body's leaning is decidedly toward the material side of life; it draws the soul after it as a matter of course. Though the soul is lofty, its association with the body can lead to its entanglement in the material world.

The soul, humanity's inner essence, is the means by which the body links to the realm of the spirit. The soul yearns always to come closer to the Source of its spiritual sustenance; a benefit that it must earn by successfully negotiating the pathways to God of this world. For this the soul needs its partner, the body. And though a person's physical nature is the dominant one in this world, the body can be "inspirited" and trained in the direction of the soul's yearning.

The familiar tug-of-war between material and spiritual reality rages throughout the week. We know it in the conflicting messages we receive from within ourselves; we recognize it in the varied cast of characters that appears on the stage of our personalities: On Sunday we are saints, on Monday, worldly-minded; on Wednesday we need to possess the latest gadgets of distraction, on Thursday, we find contentment in the blessings that we have. Unless we've worked hard to remain attuned to the yearnings of our souls, our material desires usually gain the upper hand.

The break in this ongoing struggle is Shabbat.

As Shabbat nears, the soul of everything in the world is geared to move up a rung—even many rungs—on the ladder of holiness that leads toward Godliness. But there is a stipulation to gaining entry to this spiritual channel: the body must be ready to join the soul along its journey. It must be cleansed of the mundane influences and temptations that drag on it the week through.

This is the deeper reason for our bathing in hot water on Friday afternoon, and it is the reason some people also immerse in a mikvah—a special, purifying bath. The waters counteract the damaging effects of our weeklong immersion in the marketplace, in its demands for competitiveness, high productivity and the trappings of success.

The elemental forces we employ for this spiritual cleansing are fire and water.

The "fire" element is found in the hot water we use for bathing in preparation for Shabbat; in this element of fire is contained the mystery of *like healing like*. The water's heat burns away the intractable heat of the rage and anxiety that has clung to us over the course of the week.

The "water" element is found in the mikvah, where we immerse ourselves. There we find the mystery of purity. In the short time during which our bodies remain submerged beneath the mikvah's surface, its waters of purity wash away the restlessness and feelings of alienation that have attached themselves to us during the weekdays.

With this preparation, the material and spiritual within us end their weeklong struggle for dominance; body and soul are ready to work together as true partners, to achieve the spiritual growth that Shabbat inspires. ▦

BODY AND SOUL

The extra measure of holiness that descends with the onset of Shabbat is generated Above. Everything in creation ascends to a higher spiritual plane on the seventh day without any input from below.

We humans can, however, influence the scope of that ascent on the personal level. In particular, we can affect the extent of our own advance to higher spiritual realms. The level each of us–the partnership of body and soul–reaches on Shabbat is determined by the measure of our preparation: by the degree to which we have introduced holiness into our life over the course of the week.

Even if you've immersed yourself body and soul in the mundane matters of life, with no mind toward linking with the spiritual, the extra holiness of the seventh day will increase your capacity for spiritual growth. Still, this cannot compare with the growth you can experience on Shabbat if you've made the effort to grow spiritually during the week.

(LIKUTEY HALAKHOT, EIRUVEY TECHUMIN 5:39)

SPECIAL
CLOTHING:
SUITED FOR
SHABBAT

A person should make sure to have
special garments for Shabbat. . . .
Immediately after bathing
one should don one's Shabbat garments
in honor of the day.

(SHULCHAN ARUKH, ORACH CHAIM 262:2,3)

*W*e scramble to get an education, pursue a career, set up a home, find material success and guarantee security for our old age. Along the way, we don the vestments of materialistic ambition and worldly attachments. Cut from the fabric of envy, greed and deception, these garments of which we fashion our weekday wardrobes are hardly the ones we would wear to honor the Shabbat.

The needs we acquire throughout the week are too often artificial as we grow enchanted with the notion of possessing. Even when we become conscious of the shabbiness of our wardrobes of ambition and materialistic attachment—of the spiritual emptiness they impose on our lives—not always are we able to rid ourselves of their influences day by day.

But Friday afternoon is different. With the workweek drawing to a close the time is right for changing our appearance. Washing away the weekday grime includes shedding the envy, the greed and the deceptiveness that have clung to us. These wretched garments are hardly appropriate on Shabbat, when our aim is to attire ourselves in the "clean clothing" of tranquility, contentment and integrity—the garments so beautifully suited to Shabbat. ✡

Sampling the Food: The World of Genuine Life

The custom on Friday afternoon
is to taste each of the foods
prepared for Shabbat,
to make certain that they are all
properly cooked and tasty.

(Mishnah Berurah 250:4)

Anyone who samples the foods
prepared for Shabbat
merits genuine life.

(Minhagei HaAri, Inyanei Shabbat 12)

"Genuine life"—it is the most intense joy one can experience.

The endless delight that will be our reward in the World to Come is something that, generally, we cannot feel in this world. Our physical nature prevents us from experiencing anything eternal, anything that lies outside the constraints of time and space. Bound by our bodies' spiritual insensitivity, the antennae of our five senses are unable to pick up the band on which infinity broadcasts. Even our soul, though properly tuned to the signals transmitted from the World to Come, finds its reception blocked by interference and static from this world.

In the World to Come, however, the limitations of time and space that define all corporeal reality disappear. The static of life that interferes with our reception simply does not exist there; we experience only genuine life, an existence of never-ending pleasure and boundless delight.

On Shabbat we can gain an inkling of the delight of the World to Come, even in this world. The Talmud teaches that anyone who delights in the Shabbat is rewarded with boundless blessing. This blessing makes its way into our lives through a *neshamah yeteirah*, an "added soul"—an extra measure of spiritual energy—that becomes ours on Shabbat. It is a kind of "sixth sense" that enables us to transcend the limitations of our five senses and taste of the delight of the World to Come.

Through the boundless blessing of Shabbat, our world of corporeality is imbued with an extraordinary measure of holiness. Even the physical pleasures of Shabbat—in particular the food and drink of the three Shabbat meals—provide a taste of the endless delight that awaits us in the World to Come.

By sampling our Shabbat foods on Friday afternoon, making certain they are properly cooked and spiced, we prepare ourselves, even within our finite reality, for the boundless blessing of endless, sublime delight. The measure of holiness that this blessing brings to the corporeal aspects of our existence enables us to silence the interference and static of life. Our souls are then able to receive the strong signals being broadcast from the World of Genuine Life.

THE PURPOSE OF CREATION

Everything has a purpose, and every purpose has a purpose of its own, and so on. The purpose of each facet of creation, its intended goal and completion, originates as some thought in the mind. Thus, although the purpose of anything is reached only at the end, its intended goal is in fact "closer" to the original thought than are the many steps toward implementing it, taken along the way.

The purpose of Creation was Shabbat. Although last in the order of creation, Shabbat completed and was the goal for which God brought everything else into existence. Shabbat is thus "closer" to God's original Thought than anything else that preceded it in creation.

And the purpose of Shabbat is the World to Come, the World of the Eternal Shabbat. In the World to Come, there will be nothing to obstruct or obscure our perception of God. We will all be able to point with a finger and say, *"This* is God." And *that*—our intimate association with God—is the purpose of the purpose of Creation.

(LIKUTEY MOHARAN I, 18; II, 39)

Readying the Table:
Stewards of the Queen

A person should ready the table,
spread the couches and prepare the entire house
so that upon returning home from synagogue
one will find it arranged and ordered.

(Shulchan Arukh, Orach Chaim 262:1)

On Friday afternoon, an exhilarating anticipation fills the air. We prepare a grand banquet, and set our tables with an ornate kiddush cup, with beautiful, shining candlesticks and with our finest linen and tableware—all in honor of the "Shabbat Queen," the influence of royalty that is about to grace our homes.

The Kabbalah associates this influence of royalty with *Malkhut*, the spiritual emanation, or *sefirah*, through which God's Sovereignty is disseminated in the universe. *Malkhut*, the last of the seven lower emanations, is synonymous with Shabbat, the seventh day of the week. It is *Malkhut* that interfaces with our world, affecting and being affected by human action.

Because of *Malkhut's* strong, direct connection with our world, it is subject throughout the week to the influence of forces that are outside the realm of holiness. With the arrival of Shabbat, however, *Malkhut* is released from all worldly influences. It ascends to higher realms and aligns with the other spiritual emanations; the last link in the spiritual channel for transmitting Divine blessing is in place.

The regal table that we set for the Shabbat Queen is analogous to the golden Table that stood in the northern section of the Sanctuary in the Holy Temple. The Temple Table, which held the characteristic priestly breads, linked the Jewish people to the cosmic energies of Divine blessing that draw material prosperity to the world.

Nowadays, decking out our Shabbat tables in a manner that bespeaks wealth and royalty—reflecting *Malkhut's* imminent rise to spiritual wealth—links us to those very same cosmic energies. Even more significantly, it links us to the elevated realm of *Malkhut*, Sovereignty. Preparing the royal banquet makes us members of the royal entourage, personal stewards of the Shabbat Queen. When we so identify ourselves, then Sovereignty's ascent to higher realms on Friday night is reflected in our "ascent" as well—we feel uplifted and exhilarated and aligned with the cosmic flow. שבת

PRIVATE, SECLUDED PRAYER:
EGO ON THE PYRE

How to honor it?
After washing in hot water...
one should sit attentively
and look forward
to greeting the Shabbat.

(RAMBAM, LAWS OF SHABBAT, CHAP. 30)

Every Friday,
one should examine one's actions
of the previous week and repent
for any wrongdoing.

(KITZUR SHULCHAN ARUKH #72:15)

*A*ll week long, ego is a dominant force in our lives. The traits that assert our ego, as anger, jealousy and arrogance, undermine our spiritual growth constantly. They fill us with a self-centeredness that keeps us from serving God wholeheartedly and with total commitment. Caught in their grip, we must invest tremendous effort to remain spiritually focused, to keep our inner work on track.

The most effective way to counteract the ego-based obstacles to our spiritual growth is through the "fire" of conscious self-judgment. This fire is the fervor we kindle in our hearts, the enthusiasm that animates our work on our spiritual selves. This happens when we practice *hitbodedut*—when we spend private time examining all our actions, words, emotions and thoughts through secluded meditation and personal prayer to God.

The culmination of our week's *hitbodedut* is on Friday afternoon, as Shabbat approaches. Earlier, we bathed in hot water to "burn away" the undesirable weekday influences from our bodies; similarly, immersing ourselves in *hitbodedut* burns away the spiritual impurity that ego imposes on us.

Ideally, we should have been confronting this enemy to our spiritual growth all week long, through our *hitbodedut* meditations, and now, on Friday afternoon, the battle is nearing its end. Sitting in secluded thought and prayer, we can sense in the developing calm a quieting of the ego's refrain of "I, me, mine," which comprises so much of the score of contemporary life.

Provided we have done our inner work properly, the ego loosens its hold over us. The fervor we have stirred up in our exercises of self-judgment the week through can be felt as a flame of compassion and humility, which we have kindled in our hearts. This flame melts away even the subtle remnants of our self-centeredness, readying us for the odyssey of Shabbat. ◉

SHABBAT EYES

When we view life from the vantage point of weekday eyes, we see others as having less than their true worth, while we see ourselves as something more than what we are.

But when we view life through Shabbat eyes, we recognize the image of God, both in ourselves and in others. We recognize, too, the true value of the accomplishments of others and the genuine measure of our own worth.

◆

Our tradition teaches: The facet of a person that will be privileged to partake of the World to Come is his or her humility—that fraction of oneself not intoxicated by its own importance.

Our everyday existence demands that we "make something" of ourselves and "be someone." Such ambitions prevent us from experiencing the delights of that eternal, infinite world in our own lifetime. But anyone who views life through Shabbat eyes can recognize who he really is and so build on his humility. The delight of Shabbat thus gives us a taste of the World to Come, even in this world.

(LIKUTEY MOHARAN II, 67, 72)

SONG OF SONGS: AN ORIGINAL SOUND

In some congregations it is the custom
to recite the Book of Song of Songs
on Friday afternoon
[before reciting the *Minchah* prayer].

(KITZUR SHULCHAN ARUKH #72:11)

*E*verything in God's creation has its distinctive melody, a rhythm and life-beat that it alone plays. This is especially true of humanity. Each of us has the song we sing in this world, an evolving ballad that is uniquely his or her own.

The sounds produced by the notes and chords of all the world's songs are of two kinds: "original sound" and "reflected sound." Original sound is the clear, direct sound that we create in an open space, whether with our voices or with the instruments we play. On a deeper level, it is the tone of contentment that underlies all our songs of joy and jubilation. Reflected sound is a resonance, like the echo we hear in a forest or between tall mountains. It is the tone of deficiency and imperfection underlying all our songs of sadness and despair.

Most of our personal songs, indeed most of the songs of this world, consist of reflected sound. Songs composed of original sound are rare. In word and in tone, the ballads of our lives tell mostly of disappointment and regret: of wasted talents, missed opportunities, unrealized aspirations or unrequited love.

But we don't have to be always singing the blues. We can change our tunes; in the songs of this world we can transform the sadness into joy, the despair into jubilation. The first step is to recognize the true origin of reflected sound.

Reflected sound only seems to have an independent existence, like the echoes of our voices, which seem to be coming from somewhere else far away but actually originate inside us. For just as there can be no echo without an original sound to reverberate, neither can there be a reflected sound that does not start off as original sound.

All the reflected sound in the songs of this world that express sorrow and imperfection began as the original sounds of happiness and fulfillment. These were the whispers of talent, opportunity, aspiration and love that were ours potentially. But for many these whispers never developed. Over time the realities of life caused them to be reflected back to us as the hushed and hollow echoes of so many could-have-beens. Recognizing that reflected sound stems from original sound—that despite all our setbacks, and no matter how many years and yearnings have passed, our original potential is never lost—is the first step in transforming the songs of this world.

Reciting the Book of Song of Songs just before the onset of Shabbat gives us the inspiration and the insight to attain this recognition. We can then begin to compose songs of fulfillment, the music of our own original sound.

Song of Songs is a song of a higher world. It tells not of imperfection and lack, but of love fulfilled and contentment realized:

> My beloved called out, saying to me,
>> "Arise, my darling, my beauty, and come away.
> For, see, the winter has passed,
>> the rains are over and gone.
> The blossoms have appeared in the land,
>> the time for singing has arrived,
>> and the sound of the turtledove is heard in our land."
>
> (Song of Songs 2:10-12)

We sing it in preparation for Shabbat, to remind ourselves that Shabbat, too, takes us to a world of fulfillment and contentment. Like Song of Songs, the symphony of Shabbat is fashioned of original sound—the enchanting sounds meant to remind us that our potential for wholeness, no matter how hushed, never leaves us. ◉

SHABBAT TALK

Shabbat talk is holy talk.

During the week we speak of wealth and work, of worries and wants. Our weekday talk proclaims imperfection: we often focus on what we lack or have yet to accomplish, on how we would like things to be other than as they are.

But when we speak of life's blessings and joys—the talk of Shabbat—we speak of contentment, of fulfillment. When we speak of building our souls and coming closer to God—holy talk—we speak of wholeness, of perfection. Indeed, speech itself attains perfection on Shabbat.

And when we bring Shabbat talk to the weekdays, we infuse the everyday-imperfection of our lives with a new measure of perfection.

(LIKUTEY MOHARAN I, 66:3)

PSALM 107
AND
THE MINCHAH
PRAYER:
DELIVERED
FROM DANGER

The Baal Shem Tov instituted the practice of
reciting Psalm 107 every Friday afternoon
before the *Minchah* prayer.
This psalm, *Hodu LaHashem*
("Give Thanks to God"),
speaks of the four categories of people
who must thank and praise God
for having spared them from danger.

(MEOR EINAYIM, BESHALACH)

*T*he day of Shabbat is filled with ample, unadulterated goodness and joy. To access its spirit we have to let go—releasing all our worries and problems, accepting that, for a period of twenty-five hours, everything is exactly as it should be. We have to pull back from everything that binds us and draws us to unfinished business, focusing our energy on appreciating, even celebrating, what we have in our lives. If our reflections enable us to let go, we begin to enter the spirit of Shabbat.

It is with this intention that we recite Psalm 107 along with the *Minchah* prayer. *Minchah* of Friday afternoon is the week's transitional prayer, for it carries us across the threshold that separates the weekdays from Shabbat. All the suffering that we undergo in this life, even and especially our souls' spiritual suffering, is embodied in the four categories of people referred to in this psalm who owe special thanks to God: those who have passed through a wilderness, those who were released from prison, those who were healed from illness and those who have traveled the sea.

When the springs of our spiritual vitality have dried up, when the spiritual fare that nourishes our souls no longer seems fresh, we feel lost in a wilderness. When the self-images and reputations that once defined us have become confining, when we fear moving on from positions and jobs that were once gratifying but now fail to satisfy, we feel entrapped and imprisoned. When our souls suffer dis-ease, when anxiety and melancholy plague our spirits, we feel ravaged by illness. When our minds can find no rest, when our thoughts are tossed about by the waves of confusion, we feel adrift at sea.

Over any suffering we endure we must cry out to God. Yet there are times when the week's worries and problems are so overwhelming that our hearts close and even crying is impossible. The only hope we have then is to thank and praise God with all the sincerity we can muster, for all the favors He is forever doing for us and for the wonders that surround us always. Even in the midst of our suffering, when His favors and wonders are hidden, we have to seek out and identify the ways in which God is easing our burden—and thank Him for that, too.

Recognizing God's presence in our lives and uncovering His goodness everywhere gives us the strength to begin to cry out to Him. Then we must go on crying out, trusting that He will relieve us completely of our suffering. In this trust that God will answer our pleas, we can discover the strength to let go, to release the feelings that devitalize, trap, depress or confuse us.

The psalm itself sets forth this formula. Addressing in turn each of the four categories of people who have been spared, it calls on those who have been delivered from danger and distress to give thanks and praise to God, and then to cry out to Him:

> Hodu laHashem, *Thank and praise God,*
> *for He is good; His love is eternal.*
> *Thus let those who have been delivered,*
> *those He redeemed from adversity, declare…*
> *In their distress they cried out to God,*
> *and He rescued them from their troubles.*

The ideal time for reciting this psalm is at the onset of Shabbat. During the six weekdays it is easy to become lost in the helter-skelter of life, in the turmoil of an existence of week following week in which we strive to acquire, to accomplish, to survive. Inevitably our strivings lead us to a host of difficulties and frustrations, which we can transcend only by thanking God and crying out to Him.

Emerging from the physical and spiritual dangers inherent in the weekdays, we do all we can to instill in ourselves the spirit of Shabbat. Thanking God and then crying out to Him gives us the strength to let go, to leave our worries and problems behind us, replacing them with thoughts that are only joyous and good—with the incomparable spirit of Shabbat.

> *The upright will see it and rejoice...*
> *Whoever is wise will take note of these things;*
> *they will comprehend the kindnesses of God.* 🔵

Refraining from Creative Labor:
Restoring the Sparks

The thirty-nine categories of *melakhah,*
creative labor, prohibited on Shabbat
are derived from the construction
of the Tabernacle.

(Shabbat 49b)

One of the forbidden creative labors
for which a person is liable for punishment
is sorting edible food from non-edible food,
or separating one food from another.

(Shuchan Arukh, Orach Chaim 319:1–2)

*A*t the very beginning of time, God sent forth His Light to fill the ten spiritual vessels, the *sefirot*, which He created in order to disseminate His Will in the universe. This Light was too intense for the vessels to hold and so they broke, scattering their sparks, the sparks of holiness, throughout the world. This cosmic cataclysm, known in Kabbalistic teaching as "the shattering of the vessels," gave rise to a second phase in the history of the universe, a phase that is still in progress, known as "the gathering of the sparks." During this phase, mankind's aim is to collect the fallen sparks and restore them to their original level of holiness. This is the task of *tikkun*, of world-rectification: to reconstruct a universe that has become unraveled.

The Kabbalists explain that *all* human endeavor—from the sacred commandments and rituals outlined in the Torah to the most mundane of our everyday activities—directly affects the condition of the fallen sparks. Each action, when performed in a manner that is in harmony with God's Will, gathers and elevates the sparks; when performed in a manner that is incongruous with His Will, that same action will further scatter the sparks, intensifying their "exile." Ultimately, when enough sparks have been redeemed, the broken vessels will be rectified, ushering in the era of Mashiach.

The cosmic shattering of the vessels and the scattering of the sparks found their parallel in the human realm shortly after Creation, when Adam and Eve ate from the Tree of Knowledge of Good and Evil. Just as the shattering of the vessels caused the sparks of holiness to become intermingled with and obscured by darkness, the transgression of God's Will by the first humans caused the good in creation to become intermingled with and obscured by evil. And as in the cosmic realm, it is the manner in which man acts that shapes the human realm, either effecting *tikkun* or keeping the distinction between good and evil obscured.

When Adam was created on the first Friday of Creation, he was given a single mission: to pray. This was all that was needed for him to rectify the fallen sparks and restore a world of near perfection to its former wholeness. Yet after he sinned, the obscurity and disorder that clouded creation could not be undone by prayer alone. Mankind was banished from the Garden and, for the first time, made to labor and struggle "in anguish…and by the sweat of the brow" for his sustenance (Genesis 3:17, 19). Thereafter, each act of *melakhah*, creative labor, in which Adam engaged for the sake of his livelihood represented another form of rectification—yet another form of sorting good from evil.

This task of rectification became Adam's primary legacy to all succeeding generations. Our mission in life is to gather the good, extracting it from the evil that suffuses it in all aspects of our lives. For Adam, this meant that he had to sweat and anguish over his bread; for us, it means earning our livelihood by engaging in *melakhah*—creative labor—with no small measure of anxiety and stress.

But on Shabbat all *melakhah* is forbidden. Shabbat is a time of joy and rest; it is the very essence of joy and the paradigm of rest. Were we to struggle on Shabbat, as we do throughout the week, to earn a living—to sort good from evil—our activities would violate the holiness and wholeness of the day. Indeed, it is our very detaching from our weekday activities and our refraining from all creative labor on Shabbat that effects a limited measure of the highest possible rectification—the *tikkun* that elevates good over evil, that restores fallen sparks to the realm of holiness, and that ushers in the era of Mashiach and the End of Days. ◉

SIX DAYS OF CREATION

Shabbat is sanctified time; the Tabernacle, sanctified space.

The Tabernacle is created through *melakhah*, creative labor—through acts of "doing." Shabbat is created through *menuchah*, resting from *melakhah*—through acts of "non-doing."

During the six weekdays we are to engage in the doing of our *melakhah* with the same sanctity required for constructing a Tabernacle; thus we sanctify the space of our lives.

On Shabbat, however, *melakhah* is unnecessary, even counterproductive, since it is the very non-doing on this day that effects *tikkun* in the world. We are to refrain from *melakhah* on Shabbat, just as God ceased His "creative labor" on the first Shabbat of Creation; thus we sanctify the *time* in our lives.

Then the sanctity of our personal world will parallel that of the world God fashioned at Creation.

(LIKUTEY HALAKHOT, NESIAT KAPAYIM 5:29)

ב | 2

SHABBAT: THE NIGHT

The Night:
Introduction

Our God and God of our fathers,
May You be pleased with our rest.
Sanctify us with Your mitzvahs…
Grant us Your holy Shabbat as a heritage,
And may all of Israel…rest on her.
Blessed are You, God,
Who declares the Shabbat holy.

(Friday Night Prayer)

On Friday evening, Shabbat enters our lives. The secular makes way for the sacred, and the world begins its ascent to more exalted levels of holiness. The flow of spiritual energy that fills the world on Shabbat can carry us with it toward higher levels of wholeness and holiness, to an illumination of Shabbat consciousness; but we must be receptive to spiritual energy.

The Friday evening prayer is called *Kabbalat Shabbat*. The term *kabbalah* denotes the act of receiving, indicating the receptivity that enables us to absorb the worlds of spirituality that Shabbat holds. The *kabbalah* of *Shabbat* signifies welcoming the presence of the day, sensitizing ourselves to the exalted spiritual energy that the Shabbat Queen represents, accepting it into our lives and into our beings.

Friday night, especially the *Kabbalat Shabbat* liturgy, shows the way to a state of inner openness and receptivity. Throughout the week we *take* from the universe; we reach out to assert our control over the earth and to avail ourselves of her resources. Our weekday harvest of spiritual accomplishments, too, we reap with arms outstretched, through our active striving.

In contrast, on Friday night we change to a *kabbalah* mode, a receptive framework. In this mode we allow ourselves to become vessels to receive. This entails learning to be still, to silence the cacophonous strivings of heart and mind; it entails learning to listen, attuning ourselves to the whispered call of the spirit. Above all, the receptivity of Friday night entails learning to make space within oneself to receive the *neshamah yeteirah* ("added soul"), the extra measure of spiritual energy that suffuses our lives on the seventh day.

Each of the three time frames of Shabbat—night, morning and afternoon—has its own distinct ambiance. The aura of each is associated with one of the Patriarchs. The distinctive atmosphere of Friday night is imbued with the influence of the Patriarch Yitzchak. To this time of transition into the sacred realm Yitzchak lends his characteristic qualities of sanctity, containment, introspection and receptivity.

We allude to the relevant ambiance of each time of Shabbat in the central blessing of the *Amidah* prayer that we recite then (see below). The words of this blessing are identical for all three Shabbat services—*Maariv*, *Shacharit* and *Minchah* (night, morning and afternoon)—except for the pronoun that modifies the word "Shabbat" in the final verse before the prayer's closing blessing.

> *Our God and God of our fathers, may You be pleased with our rest. Sanctify us with Your mitzvahs…and may all of Israel…rest on her.*

In the Friday night *Maariv* prayer we refer to Shabbat using a feminine pronoun: "…may all of Israel…rest on *her*." In the Shabbat morning *Shacharit* prayer we switch to a masculine reference: "…may all of Israel…rest on *him*." And in the *Minchah* prayer of Shabbat afternoon we switch again, referring to Shabbat as an integrated plural: "…may all of Israel…rest on *them*."

The Kabbalists tell us that we, male and female alike, receive the feminine aspect of our *neshamah yeteirah* on Friday night and the masculine aspect on Shabbat morning. At the time of the *Minchah* prayer on Shabbat afternoon, we move to a complete integration.

We invoke the feminine aspect of our "added soul" on Friday night both by welcoming the Shabbat Queen with the *Kabbalat Shabbat* prayer and by receiving the *Shekhinah*, the "feminine face" of the Divine, in Whose honor the Friday night meal is held. One way in which this dimension of our *neshamah yeteirah* is manifest is in the embracing of intimacy that has made this first meal of Shabbat a time for family and friends.

We discover, too, traces of this archetypal feminine in those qualities of Yitzchak that give Friday night its particular ambiance—in the stepping back from the world and the containment we experience as we bring an end to work; in the receptivity we unlock in ourselves through the *Kabbalat Shabbat* prayer; and in the deepened reflectiveness by which we appreciate the wonders and blessings of life, which comes with sanctifying the day by reciting the kiddush at our Shabbat tables.

CANDLE LIGHTING:
ENLIGHTENED TRUTH

As dusk nears, one should remind
the members of one's household:
"Kindle the Shabbat lights…."
Some are of the opinion that
a person is required to extend
a part of the week to Shabbat
(accepting upon oneself the holiness of Shabbat
before the actual day of Shabbat arrives).

(SHULCHAN ARUKH, ORACH CHAIM 260:2; 261:2)

Shabbat holds all the intensity of the essence of truth. Our Sages were in awe of the sanctity of Shabbat. "Even those who are unlearned find it virtually impossible to tell a lie on that day," they commented, and indeed this was the case in the times of the Talmud.

Even today, Shabbat is the time for seeing past the comfortable "weekday-truths" with which most of us cushion our lives. These are the partial truths we construct to help us avoid taking responsibility for the whole of who we are. It is never easy to face the inconsistencies we recognize in ourselves. Although we may think of ourselves as compassionate and caring, if put to the test we might be disturbed to find ourselves responding insensitively. Accepting the whole truth can be painful.

Faced with the discrepancy between our principles and our actions, we often opt for a partial truth. We may tell ourselves that it would have required a superhuman effort to respond other than as we did, or that for reasons beyond our control, we were acting out of character at that moment. These rationalizations are far more comfortable to live with than is accepting that we are not as caring or as selfless as we would like to believe.

While this limited honesty that dominates our "weekday characteristics" enables us to navigate around the sharp edges of our self-images, it also keeps us from the self-awareness we need in order to grow, an awareness that can exist only when we acknowledge the whole picture, inconsistencies and all. Unless we are honest with ourselves about who we really are, open to examining under light every element of truth, we cannot heal the fragmented shards of our personalities.

The most effective light for conducting this examination, for revealing and healing the half-truths that eat away at our souls, is the light of Shabbat. As the Sages of the Talmud recognized, its radiance reflects nothing less than the illumination of the whole truth. In the calm that is Shabbat, in the peacefulness that settles over our homes and into our beings when we pull back from all weekday busyness, we can find comfort and security. This enables us to let go of the defenses and rationalizations that are our "comforters" during the week. Truth then becomes more apparent, the limitations imposed upon us by our limited honesty more obvious.

And while the illumination of Shabbat shines throughout the day, our initial perception of it comes through the tangible light of the Shabbat candles. We usher in the Shabbat by lighting two candles late on Friday afternoon. In kindling these lights shortly before the actual onset of the holy day, we "expand" the Shabbat, so that the light of its holiness may extend into the week; that the radiance of its truth may touch and heal all the fragmentation and the weekday-truths of our lives.

Then, taking a moment to gaze upon the Shabbat candles, allowing ourselves to embrace the truth made palpable by their radiance, we too are embraced by the light of Shabbat. In the wholeness of its truth we can find the honesty to dismantle all our partial truths; we can absorb the sanctity that makes lying, even to ourselves, virtually impossible. In its healing embrace we can cultivate the self-awareness and summon the courage to take responsibility for the whole of who we are.

ILLUMINATING THE TEMPLE

Tradition teaches: Shabbat is the source of the Light that illumines the Holy Temple and with it the entire world. This is why observing the Shabbat enables us to open our eyes and see deep within, into our own inner temples: Shabbat affords us the opportunity to assess our direction in life and evaluate our inner strengths. And observing Shabbat enhances our ability to focus on our relationship with God, as we draw close to the innermost point of Truth.

(LIKUTEY MOHARAN II, 67)

THE KABBALAT SHABBAT PRAYER (1): THROUGH THE GATEWAY

The Talmud teaches:
As Shabbat drew near the Sages
would don their finest garments
and say to one another,
"Let us go out to greet the Shabbat Queen."

(SHABBAT 119A)

It is customary to begin Friday evening's
Kabbalat Shabbat ("Greeting the Shabbat") prayer
with six psalms (Psalms 95-99 and Psalm 29),
one for each day of the week.
This originated with Rabbi Moshe Cordovero,
a leading figure among the 16th century
Kabbalists of Safed.

(SEDER HA YOM)

When Shabbat arrives it infuses the universe with increased spirituality as an unimpeded flow of spiritual energy descends into the world. This energy initiates the spiritual ascent of everything in creation to higher levels of wholeness and holiness.

For humankind, Shabbat means the capacity for greater spiritual intensity. This wholeness holds the potential for heightened insightfulness of the mind and heightened sensitivity of the heart, the vehicles for spiritual uplifting.

In order for anything to ascend to a higher level of spirituality, it must first pass through the entryway that leads from one level to the next. At the entryway to each level there stands a "gatekeeper" that attempts to prevent an infusion of spirit and deny greater spiritual perception, a gatekeeper that goes by the name "Illusion." To pass through the gate, one must first vanquish the keeper that would bar one's entry.

Illusion has many faces. At each level it appears as precisely that insurmountable obstacle one hoped never to encounter. For each person it appears as just that intractable issue one wished never to address. Sometimes illusion takes the form of distractions of the mind; at other times it takes the form of agitation of the heart. At all times it mirrors the fiery, ever-turning sword God placed at the entryway to Eden to guard the path to the Tree of Life.

The individual life of every human being is a microcosm that reflects a universal process. The key, therefore, to vanquishing the illusion at each spiritual level and to unlocking the holiness that lies beyond, lies in human hands. In order to vanquish the illusions that drag us down, we need to make God's greatness known in the world, to become aware of the Godliness that suffuses all existence and to share that recognition with everything in creation.

It is with this intention that we recite the psalms of the *Kabbalat Shabbat* prayer that ushers in the Shabbat. The theme that is common to all these psalms is the greatness and glory of God. Thus we greet the Shabbat Queen declaring:

> *For a great God is the Lord,*
>> *and a great King over all heavenly forces* (Psalm 95).

> *Relate His glory among the peoples,*
>> *among all the nations His wonders...*
> *Declare among the peoples: "God reigns!"* (Psalm 96).

> *Let the heavens proclaim His justness,*
>> *let all the peoples perceive His glory* (Psalm 97).

When we connect to the words that flow from our lips as we declare God's greatness, when we allow their meaning to suffuse our souls, prayer becomes the vehicle for self-transformation that it is meant to be. Declaring His glory to ourselves and to the universe awakens in us a deeper recognition of the Godliness that quickens all of life.

In the awe and wonder of this deeper recognition, the distractions of our minds are stilled and the agitation of our hearts calmed. The erstwhile-intractable illusions that would bar our entry to any new spiritual insight have been shattered; the once indomitable gatekeeper that would bar our way to a higher branch on the Tree of Life has been vanquished. 🕎

KNOWING GOD

When we experience the holiness of Shabbat, we attain the highest levels of *daat*, of knowing God. And the highest level of this *daat*-consciousness that we can achieve is the realization that God is altogether incomprehensible—that we really know nothing at all.

(LIKUTEY MOHARAN II, 83)

THE KABBALAT SHABBAT PRAYER (2): THE VOICE OF DIVINE REPLY

Rabbi Yitzchak Luria
(the preeminent 16th century Kabbalist
of Safed known as the holy Ari)
would greet the Shabbat out in the field.
Facing westward, the Ari would wait
for the moment of sunset and then,
with eyes closed and with the reverence
and awe of one standing before a king,
he would recite Psalm 29:
"A psalm of David: Ascribe unto God. . . ."

(MINHAGEI HAARI, INYANEI SHABBAT 17)

*T*he flow of spiritual energy that fills the world as Shabbat enters our lives has the power to bring us along with it toward higher levels of wholeness and holiness, to an illumination of Shabbat consciousness—provided we are receptive to its spiritual energy.

This receptiveness requires that we first free ourselves of our weekday worries and difficulties, and replace the concerns that burden our minds with thoughts that are positive and joyous. Thus as part of our Shabbat preparations, at the divide that separates the weekdays from Shabbat, we recited Psalm 107, the "*Hodu*" psalm. We thanked and praised God for the good in our lives; this enabled us to put the week—its disappointments *and* its successes—into perspective.

Yet this alone is insufficient to sensitize our hearts and attune our minds to receive the flow of spiritual energy that Shabbat brings. Often the only way to foster and refine this receptiveness is to cry out repeatedly to God for the things we lack and for the things we seek yet to achieve. Thus in the *Hodu* psalm we also cried out to Him for the courage to be open as well as the wisdom to think only positive and joyous thoughts.

Once we have approached God in this manner we are only a step away from having crossed to the other side of the week's divide, and we are ready to chant Psalm 29. This, say the Sages, signifies our official reception of the Shabbat: The words of the *Hodu* psalm have brought us to a state of receptivity; declaring God's greatness with each of the first five psalms of the *Kabbalat Shabbat* prayer has checked the illusions that might prevent our spiritual advance. With the recitation of Psalm 29 we are able to vanquish these illusions altogether, and when we do this we will be ready to receive the inflow of spirit that illumines us with the holiness of Shabbat.

> A *psalm of* David:
>> Ascribe unto God, O children of the strong,
> Ascribe unto God glory and might.
> Ascribe unto God the honor due His Name…
>> The voice of God is upon the waters…
>> The voice of God issues with power.
>> The voice of God issues with splendor.
>> The voice of God splinters cedars…
>> The voice of God hews with flames of fire.
>> The voice of God convulses the wilderness…
>> The voice of God frightens the hinds and
>>> lays the forests bare.

In ascribing to God glory and might and the honor due His Name, we are praising Him as we did in the Hodu psalm—but here there is a difference. Our earlier words of praise and thanksgiving enabled us to moan and cry out to God; they served as a means for giving voice to a heart so overwhelmed that even crying was impossible. Having completed our preparations for Shabbat, our praise and thanksgiving have become the voice of prayer—the voice that issues to all of existence its sevenfold declaration of God's greatness: *upon the waters; with power; with splendor; splintering cedars; hewing with flames of fire; convulsing the wilderness; frightening hinds and laying the forest bare.*

With the gatekeeper vanquished, the entryway to a higher level of spirit beckons us across. As we pass through, our senses encounter mystery: a "voice" other than our own that declares the *seven Voices of God.*

In the stillness born of our receptivity we can detect the Divine reply to our cries, issued earlier in the Hodu psalm. God is responding, as it were, through the *seven Voices*. With each declaration He transmits to this world the illumination embedded in that *Voice*. This transmission of spiritual energy on Shabbat fills the world, as it fills us, with a greater measure of holiness and wholeness. 🕎

LEKHA DODI
HYMN (1):
A RECEPTION
FOR THE BRIDE

While still standing in the field
to greet the Shabbat,
the Ari would follow Psalm 29 with the words:
"Enter, O bride! Enter, O bride!
Enter, O bride, the Shabbat Queen!"

(MINHAGEI HAARI, INYANEI SHABBAT 17)

*T*here are times when the truest act of giving is to receive, when the truest form of doing is not to do at all.

Shabbat is the channel for all the blessing and sustenance we enjoy throughout the week. All the material good for which we labor every other day of the week in fact derives from this one day—Shabbat—when we refrain from labor.

The Biblical paradigm for this is the manna that sustained the Jews in the wilderness. It fell daily, enough for one day at a time, but only on the six weekdays. The manna never fell on Shabbat. Yet Shabbat was the spiritual channel that linked the six weekdays to the supernal wellspring of sustenance that came in the form of manna.

Every day of the week has its own spiritual channel for transmitting sustenance to the world. Once a week, on the seventh day, these spiritual channels converge within the channel of Shabbat. The influence of Shabbat fills them with sustenance so that, one by one throughout the week, each day's channel brings the world that day's sustenance.

On Shabbat, however, this daily distribution by which God's sustains the world the week through is interrupted. The spiritual channels cannot function in two modes simultaneously; at the time they are *receiving* sustenance they cannot be passing it on. On Shabbat all spiritual channels, including Shabbat's channel, are receiving. The channel of Shabbat thus never gives sustenance to the world on its day.

This is why, although no manna fell on Shabbat, it was through the very act of *receiving* that Shabbat facilitated the *giving* of sustenance the rest of the week. Even today, although we refrain from working on Shabbat and earning a living, it is this very cessation of work that brings success to all our weekday labor. Through *not doing*, Shabbat facilitates the *doing* that brings us blessing and sustenance the rest of the week.

The place for seeking one's livelihood through the week is out in the "field." As if we were indeed working in a field, the workplace exposes us to the elements—to the onslaught of circumstances and attitudes that undermine the world we create for ourselves and our families within our homes. We do not always succeed in fending off the outside influences that compel us to compromise even our most cherished values and beliefs.

In order to separate the week's sustenance from the pull and pressure of the field—to draw its blessing inward, the Kabbalists of Safed made it their custom to go out to the fields to recite the *Kabbalat Shabbat* and welcome in the Shabbat bride.

When we ready ourselves and our homes for Shabbat, we bring completion and closure to the workweek. We reclaim all the parts of our selves that we had sent out into the world to negotiate our everyday existence. With the onset of Shabbat we bring all work (*melakhah*), all association with the week, to a standstill. Our preparations and prayers have fortified us with the deeper understanding that the sustenance we strive for throughout the week can never be taken, only received—through *not doing*. By reciting the *Kabbalat Shabbat* we return one final time to the "outerness" of the field—"Come my beloved, let us go out to the field"—to welcome and gather in the week's blessing: "Enter, O bride. Enter, O bride. Enter, O bride, the Shabbat Queen." 🔹

LEKHA DODI HYMN (2): KINDLING THE INNER MENORAH

The version of the *Lekha Dodi*
("Come My Beloved to Greet the Bride")
hymn that has been adopted universally
as part of the *Kabbalat Shabbat* prayer
was composed by another of the Safed kabbalists,
Rabbi Shlomo Alkabetz.

(LIKUTEY MAHAREI'AKH 2, KABBALAT SHABBAT)

God's blessing to the seventh day is His Divine Light, which shines brighter on Shabbat than on any other day (*Bereishit Rabbah* 11:2). Enthralled by its radiance, we cross the threshold into the week's holiest day singing of our longing to welcome this Light as it flows into our souls:

> Come let us welcome the Shabbat,
>> for it is the source of blessing;
> From earliest antiquity she was honored—
>> last in creation, first in intention.
>
> Come my beloved to greet the bride,
>> let us greet the countenance of Shabbat.
>
> (From the *Lekha Dodi* Hymn)

Many follow this with the recital of a passage from the *Zohar* as a bridge from *Kabbalat Shabbat* to the *Maariv* prayer. These words of mystical teaching, known as the *Ke'gavne* prayer, paint for us a portrait of the "countenance of Shabbat" as the glowing radiance of God's Presence, the *Shekhinah*. Yet, the *Zohar* tells us, the countenance of Shabbat is also the radiance that characterizes *our* faces once we've been crowned with a *neshamah yeteirah* (an "added soul")—the unique soul of Shabbat:

> Her countenance glows with a heavenly light.
> Below, She crowns herself with the holy people,
>> and they in turn all crown themselves with new souls.
> Then they begin their prayers by blessing Her,
>> joyously and with radiant faces,
>> declaring: Bless God, the blessed One.
>
> (Zohar II, 135b)

The Kabbalah likens the head to the seven-branched Menorah of the Holy Temple. The head's seven orifices—two eyes, two ears, two nostrils and a mouth—parallel the seven oil lamps.

The priests were required to remove the ashes and change the wicks of the Temple Menorah, and fuel it with only pure, virgin olive oil. The light of the seven oil lamps illuminated the "face of the Menorah" and caused it to glow.

We must tend to our own menorahs with no less care: We must clean and purify our minds constantly through purifying our seven lamps, guarding both what enters and what emanates from these orifices. We must fuel them only with the pure intellect of the mind.

When we greet the Shabbat Queen, her radiant countenance kindles the pure intellect of our menorahs with a fiery enthusiasm, causing them to burn with a radiant glow. If we nurture this enthusiasm and fan it with all the intensity of spiritual devotion and sacred celebration of Shabbat, it will flare up inside us in the form of an inextinguishable fervor born of God's closeness. Our faces will then shine as brightly as did the face of the Menorah that stood in the Holy Temple.

THE
SHABBAT
PSALM:
THE BLISS OF
A HIGHER WORLD

The Ari would conclude *Kabbalat Shabbat*
by reciting Psalms 92 and 93.

(MINHAGEI HAARI, INYANEI SHABBAT 17)

Mizmor shir leyom haShabbat—
A psalm, a song for the Shabbat day.
It is good to give thanks to God,
to sing praise to Your Name;
to tell, O Most High, of Your kindnesses...

(PSALM 92)

*T*here is nothing that brings greater sweetness to our souls than thanking and praising God. In the World to Come our expanded awareness and recognition of the Holy One will find expression in our extolling His greatness and proclaiming our appreciation for all His kindnesses. This is the bliss that awaits us in the next world.

Fortunately, we do not have to wait until we leave this world to experience that bliss. We can gain a sense of this intense joy once each week, on Shabbat, for this day is a sampling of the World to Come. With the setting of the sun, we received the Shabbat Queen and welcomed into our beings the light of her countenance in the form of the *neshamah yeteirah* ("added soul") that graces us. We are ready now to conclude the *Kabbalat Shabbat* with yet another declaration of praise and thanks to God.

We entered Shabbat with the praise and thanksgiving of the *Hodu* psalm, which enabled us to cry out to God; then we advanced to the praise and thanksgiving of the *Kabbalat Shabbat* psalms, which culminated in the sevenfold declaration of God's greatness; we are now ready to offer the praise and thanksgiving of the soul itself, whose sweetness bespeaks the bliss of a higher world. Inspired by this unparalleled good, we raise our voices in song: "A psalm, a song for the Shabbat day. It is *good* to give thanks to God, to sing praise..."

◆

The Midrash (*Bereishit Rabbah* 22:13) relates:

> Soon after Cain emerged from the heavenly court, where he had been tried for murdering his brother Abel, he encountered his father. "How did you fare?" Adam asked his son.
>
> "I repented and was pardoned," Cain answered with relief.
>
> Adam was startled. "If only I had known earlier of the great power of repentance [I too would have hastened to repent]!" It was then that Adam proclaimed: "A psalm, a song for the Shabbat day."

What was it that made Adam think of Shabbat when he learned of the efficacy of *teshuvah*, repentance, and realized that his sin too could be pardoned through his repentance?

When we transgress the Will of God, we upset the tranquil balance of our own lives. And the farther we stray from God's Will the more disquiet and dis-ease we experience. But when we repent sincerely, our agitation vanishes. Turmoil and tension are replaced with a deep sense of tranquility.

This is the spirit of Shabbat; it is the peacefulness we find when we refrain from all creative labor, the serenity that settles over our homes and into our beings when we pull back from all weekday busyness and activity. The moment Adam learned that *teshuvah* would free him of his disquiet, he associated repentance with Shabbat; the tranquility that *teshuvah* brings and the serenity that is the dividend of Shabbat are one. After cleansing our bodies, hearts and minds, after kindling the candles, after calling out to God in prayer and being called by Him, we too proclaim: "*Mizmor shir leyom haShabbat*—A psalm, a song for the Shabbat day." ⬤

THE MAARIV PRAYER: "UNCREATING" CREATION

The *Vayechulu* passage is recited
in the *Maariv* prayer of Shabbat.

(SHULCHAN ARUKH, ORACH CHAIM 268:1)

Rabbi Hamnuna taught:
When reciting the verses of *Vayechulu*
as part of the *Maariv* prayer
one becomes God's collaborator
in Creation.

(SHABBAT 119B)

*T*he highest purpose of humankind is to be filled with an awareness of God, fully conscious of the immediacy of His presence everywhere. Before the beginning, when no universe yet existed, everything that God intended to create was entirely one with the Source of All Being. That essential reality has never changed. Lest we think that God exists apart from ourselves, this impression of separateness is nothing but illusion; man, the universe and everything in it exist only within God's Unity.

When we achieve this awareness—the recognition that there never was a true separation between man and God at all—then humanity can earn its way back to a unity and oneness with its Creator.

To the extent that we succeed in dispelling the illusion of separateness, the countless other forms in creation achieve their ultimate purpose, just as we do. We might say, therefore, that God created human beings in order that we should return the universe to the state of unity and oneness with God that existed before the beginning—that we should consciously *"uncreate"* our selves and all the other forms of creation.

> Vayechulu: *Thus heaven and earth and all their legions were finished; on the seventh day God finished (vayechal) the work that He had been doing. He thus desisted on the seventh day from all the work that He had done. And God blessed the seventh day and declared it holy, because on it God abstained from all the work that He had created to do* (Genesis 2:1-3).

When we read these verses according to their simple meaning—with the words *vayechulu* and *vayechal* translated literally, as "finished"—we find in them an account of what took place long ago, at the beginning of Creation: On the first Shabbat God ceased all His work; the work of creating heaven and earth and all that they contain was finished. The *Vayechulu* passage is part of the narrative of Creation. It is the account of what the Kabbalists refer to as "creation of something out of nothing."

This is Torah read as history.

Our understanding of the passage is expanded and enhanced by associating the words *vayechulu* and *vayechal* with the word *tachlit*, an etymologically related term that implies the attainment of "completeness" or "ultimate purpose." When viewed in this light, the passage of *Vayechulu* describes not only the past but the present as well:

> *Thus heaven and earth and all their legions fulfill their* ultimate purpose; *through the seventh day God brings* completeness *to the work that He did.*

Every week on the seventh day, all of creation has an opportunity to experience a sense of having achieved its ultimate purpose—that state of completeness in which everything recognizes its unity and oneness with God. The *Vayechulu* passage tells the story of *uncreating*, an act the Kabbalists refer to as "the transformation of something into Nothing."

This is Torah read as dynamic process.

By reading this passage as dynamic process we discover too that Shabbat is not merely a time when everything in creation can experience a sense of having achieved its ultimate purpose; Shabbat is also the *means* by which we, and all of creation along with us, achieve this. God brings completeness to the universe *"through* the seventh day"—through the extra measure of holiness that fills the world on Shabbat.

At the heart of the holiness of Shabbat is an immediacy of God's presence in the world. By ceasing from all weekday work and focusing instead on the mitzvahs—the laws, customs and prayers—which make us spiritually sensitive and receptive, we are better able to sense God's presence in every aspect of our lives. We can know, as the Psalmist declares, that the whole world is full of God.

This amplified awareness of God leads to a diminished absorption in our selves. It enables us to experience a spiritual state in which we are so focused on God's presence that we are no longer conscious of our own. By "forgetting" ourselves in this manner, we *uncreate* our separate selves. In this state of self-obscurement, all that exists is God. We can recognize, if but fleetingly, our unity and oneness with the Source of All Being—turning our *something* back into Nothing.

On Shabbat the immediacy of God's presence makes it that much easier for us to forget our own separate existence. It is thus the ideal time to experience a sense of having achieved our ultimate purpose. Our very first opportunity on Shabbat to experience this is when we recite the *Vayechulu* passage in the *Maariv* prayer. The words of prayer, as conduits of spiritual energy, are the instruments of Creation. They do not merely relate an event; they generate it (see Section 3: "Reading the Torah Portion").

To the extent that we absorb ourselves in the words of *Vayechulu*, such that we are no longer aware of our selves, we become the channels through which the words of the prayer themselves influence creation. Through our reuniting with the Creator, through recognizing that there was never a true separation at all, "heaven and earth and all their legions fulfill their ultimate purpose" as well. Thus we become God's partners in *uncreating* and His collaborators in creating the most perfect of universes. ●

GOD'S PARTNERS IN CREATION

By following the Creator's work schedule—doing our *melakhah*-work during the six days of the week and refraining from all creative labor on the seventh—we attest to our belief that God created the world in six days and ceased His "work" of creating on the Shabbat. This demonstration of faith is the essence of the restfulness, tranquility and harmony—the *menuchah*—that was absent from the world until the first Shabbat of Creation, the very *menuchah* that continues to bring wholeness and blessing to the work of all the weekdays of our lives. Thus through our faith, we become God's partners in Creation.

(LIKUTEY MOHARAN II, 8)

SHALOM ALEIKHEM:
GREETING ANGELS

Greetings, O ministering angels,
angels of the Exalted One...
May your coming be for peace,
O angels of peace...Bless me for peace,
O angels of peace...
May your departure be for peace,
O angels of peace...

(SHALOM ALEIKHEM SONG)

*A*ngels—the channels of spiritual energy to which we open ourselves and which we lay open in our mystical journey called life; those nonphysical, undetectable powers that administer every event in the world, from the fall of mighty empires to the growth of every blade of grass (Bereishit Rabbah 10:7).

Angels—the messengers of God, sent to carry out the Divine Will in the world; those agents from the spiritual dimension that appear in varied forms, whether as ordinary human beings, as the translucent figures that bore God's Throne in Ezekiel's vision, or as the gentle, guiding hand of intuition.

To these angels—these celestial beings so unfathomable yet palpable to the instinct—we direct our song: *Greetings, O ministering angels, angels of the Exalted One...*

The Talmud relates:

> No one returns home alone from the prayers of Shabbat eve. Two angels, one minister of good fortune and one minister of misfortune, escort each of us. If when we arrive we find the candles lit and the table set, the angel of good declares, "May it be this way again next week," and the angel of misfortune begrudgingly responds, "Amen." But if we arrive home to a dark house with nothing prepared in honor of the Shabbat, the angel of misfortune declares, "May it be this way again next week," and the angel of good perforce responds, "Amen" (Shabbat 119b).

We humans are unique. While everything else in the world is either physical or spiritual, we human beings are the one creation in which these two altogether different elements are allied: the spirit of the soul and the substance of the body. This union leaves us singularly positioned to affect both the physical and the spiritual realm; our physical actions influence the spiritual forces—the angels.

Although in this world human beings stand on a lower spiritual plane than do angels, the human soul is rooted in a place that is loftier than the haven of angelic forces. If we but cultivate and harness our souls' spiritual powers, we garner influence over the angels to bring them to channel greater blessing into the world.

With our Friday preparations we have realized those powers. From our bathing in hot water and donning fine clothing to preparing our homes and readying our tables in honor of Shabbat, we've infused spirit in the physical and material elements of our lives. And these same preparations that have readied us for a higher perception of God have likewise enabled the angels and assisted them in investing every detail of this world, even each blade of grass, with greater spiritual energy. Without exception, in ways we cannot begin to comprehend, our preparations have elevated and inspirited every facet of creation.

And so as Shabbat makes its appearance, when the wellsprings of spiritual bounty and blessing are bursting forth, the angels accompany us home from the synagogue. We approach our Shabbat tables—set bountifully for a grand banquet, with candles burning brightly—and from there engage the spiritual forces that have entered our homes.

With the authority of souls empowered, we call on the spiritual forces to channel even greater blessing: *Greetings, O ministering angels, angels of the Exalted One...Bless me...O angels of peace.*

Seeing that we have put the previous week's bounty to good use, the angels declare, "May it be this way again next week." May this order, this beauty, this indwelling of spirit and peace, return next week.

To ensure that this indeed happens, these channels of spirit expand so that in the week ahead even greater bounty can come our way, and can, through us, be disseminated to all of creation. ◉

THE FRAGRANCE
OF MYRTLES:
HORS D'OEUVRES
FOR THE SOUL

Standing at the Shabbat table,
the Ari would take two bunches of myrtle twigs,
one in each hand:
one representing the Biblical term *zachor* (remember),
to "remember" the Shabbat,
and one representing the term *shamor* (guard),
to "keep" its laws and customs.
Bringing the two bunches together,
he would recite the blessing over them
and inhale their fragrance.

(MINHAGEI HAARI, INYANEI SHABBAT 17)

*T*he human soul requires nourishment no less than does the body; else it will wither and languish. Yet unless we have invested serious effort in purifying ourselves and harnessing our physical desires, the food we eat tends to provide sustenance that is physical rather than spiritual; it nourishes our bodies but not our souls. In fact it rouses our inclination for the material while it lulls into slumber the predilections of the spirit.

Genuine soul food, according to the Talmud (Berakhot 43b), is fragrance; the sustenance our souls derive from this world comes to us through the sense of smell. The nutrients in the foods we ingest enter our bodies together with substances that must be eliminated. The fragrances and aromas we inhale, on the other hand, enter the body in a pure form and are linked with no waste products. When we breathe in this altogether spiritual matter, our souls, lofty and inherently pure, gain nourishment from substances pure and spiritual.

The only way physical food can become spiritual sustenance is if we focus on its spiritual dimensions— through ensuring that it is kosher, reciting blessings, and eating with the conscious intent to use the energy this food provides to strengthen our devotions. The more spiritual our motivation when we eat, the more spiritually nourishing our food becomes.

Eating for spirituality can be accomplished most effectively on Shabbat. The more relaxed atmosphere that prevails at the Shabbat table lends itself to reflection and enables us to focus on the subtler, spiritual aspects of eating. We are better able to tune in to the food's vital essence, not merely to the physical gratification it provides.

Beyond this reflection and attentiveness that accompany the way we eat, the meals of Shabbat are by their very nature spiritual sustenance. The pleasure they give is of a higher order, a pleasure that prompted the prophet Isaiah to call the Shabbat *oneg*, "a delight" (Isaiah 58:13). The Sages tell us that through eating the Shabbat foods we experience a "taste" of the Garden of Eden. Their unique aroma, a mark of their essence, is something that cannot be duplicated under other circumstances.

> *"Why do the foods of Shabbat smell so delicious?"* the emperor of Rome asked Rabbi Yehoshua ben Chanina.*
>
> *"We Jews have a special seasoning," explained Rabbi Yehoshua. "It's called Shabbat. It gives our foods a wonderful aroma."*
>
> *"Surely you'll give me some of this seasoning," said the Emperor.*
>
> *"I'm sorry, but that's impossible," replied Rabbi Yehoshua. "The 'Shabbat seasoning' is available only to those who observe the Shabbat" (Shabbat 119a).*

The fragrance of myrtle (or some other aromatic herb or spice) that we inhale at our Shabbat table serves as the hors d'oeuvre for an entire meal of spiritual sustenance. This vital essence adds the attentiveness we need to transform our eating into a conscious act; it rouses our predilections for Shabbat's extensive spiritual menu. Inhaling the fragrance whets our appetites for the main course—the *delight* we savor by feasting on aromatic foods flavored with the "remembering" and the "keeping" of the Shabbat ritual laws and customs. This is the "*zachor*-and-*shamor* seasoning" of Shabbat. שבת

THE KIDDUSH: MIND OVER TIME

The Torah commands that we sanctify
the Shabbat with words, as it is written,
"Remember the day of Shabbat to sanctify it"—
remember it with words of praise
and sanctification.
And one must remember it at its onset,
with the kiddush.

(RAMBAM, LAWS OF SHABBAT, CHAP. 29)

The Sages established
that this act of "remembering"
be done over a cup of wine.

(KITZUR SHULCHAN ARUKH #77:1)

*T*ime...other than perhaps money, there is nothing we find ourselves short of more often than time. We are forever searching for just a few extra minutes, another hour or two, even an additional day in the week.

The fact is that time insinuates itself far too much in our lives. We have cut-off dates and deadlines to meet, trains and planes to catch, calendars covered with appointments and things we need to do; strict schedules legislate our work time, our vacation time, our free time. What we could use a good deal more of is not time but *freedom* from time.

Bondage to time has defined humanity right from the start—indeed, it came into existence with the beginning of Creation; and each of us individually "runs out of time" when he leaves this world. But until that moment, the degree to which the constrictions of time govern our lives is in fact ours to determine and manage.

The key to true time management is *awareness*. Time is not an entity of our own making, but our experience of time and the specific constraints it places on our lives are often the constructs of our minds. The more consciously *aware* we are, the less we experience the oppressive control of time.

Generally, we gauge the passage of time according to the yardstick of our everyday waking state. In the unconsciousness of the dream state, however, time inhabits an altogether different dimension; then we can live through the events of a lifetime in a matter of minutes. Likewise at the other extreme, when we find ourselves in a state of intense alertness, time is hardly apparent. Hours can pass by in what will seem to us to be no more than a few minutes.

We spend most of our lives at neither of these extremes, but hovering around a state of everyday perception. Yet during certain special moments it happens that we gain some insight into the sacred nature of things, and with the rearrangement of priorities fostered by that heightened state of awareness, we manage, at least temporarily, to free ourselves of our enslavement to time. Nevertheless, if we do not take full advantage of these opportunities to tune in to the spiritual side of life, the opposite may occur and our appreciation for the spiritual might wane. In the frenzied pursuit of our goals we might enslave ourselves to the high-tech innovations of our instant society, thereby relinquishing to time ever more control over our lives.

Observing Shabbat—leaving behind the week's schedules, obligations and commitments; replacing outwardly directed activity with inwardly focused receptivity—weakens time's hold on us. The relaxed and reflective atmosphere of Shabbat offers clear evidence that it is our state of mind that governs our perception of time. This is one reason the Sages associated the Shabbat with the eternal world, calling Shabbat a "preview of the World to Come," of the freedom that comes with loosening the bonds of time.

Our first taste of this freedom comes when we recite the Shabbat kiddush. All its words proclaim God's sanctification of time. Through its words, too, we "remember the day of Shabbat to sanctify it"; we effect our own sanctification of time by freeing ourselves from its bonds.

Drinking the kiddush wine is intrinsically bound up with our remembering of the Shabbat. The wine of kiddush is wine drunk in holiness. Rather than dulling our awareness and strengthening the stranglehold of time, the kiddush wine awakens in us a spirit of reflectiveness and joy. This World-to-Come sense of total freedom from the fetters of time is our gateway into the higher consciousness of Shabbat. שבת

REMEMBERING THE SHABBAT

Judaism ascribes no specific names to any of the six weekdays. We have no Sunday, Monday or Tuesday; nor is there a Wednesday, a Thursday or even a Friday.

The Torah directs us to "remember the day of Shabbat"—we are to remember it from the very first day of the week. Thus we refer to the weekdays only in terms of their places relative to Shabbat, as "the first day of Shabbat," "the second day of Shabbat"... and so on, through "the sixth day of Shabbat," or "Shabbat eve." It is Shabbat that defines and binds the other six days of the week.

(LIKUTEY MOHARAN II, 39)

Lechem Mishneh—Double Loaves:
An Aura of
Wholeness

At the Shabbat meals one should
break bread over two loaves,
as it is written:
"they gathered *lechem mishneh*—
a double portion" (Exodus 16:22). . . .
This was Rav Kahana's custom:
He would recite the blessing
over two whole loaves
and then cut one of them,
slicing a large piece...
since that indicates one's relish
for the Shabbat meal.

(Tur, Orach Chaim 274)

*T*he manna, the heavenly bread that sustained the Jewish people throughout their journey in the wilderness, fell in daily allotments. Each Friday, however, a double portion of manna fell. On that day the head of each Jewish household would gather two portions: one for Friday's meals, the other for the meals he and his family would eat on Shabbat.

We recall that double portion of manna by reciting the blessing and breaking bread over two whole loaves of challah at each Shabbat meal. Our setting the table with *lechem mishneh* ("double loaves" of challah) represents all the spiritual qualities of manna; it expresses too our recognition of the need to infuse moral and spiritual values into the way we conduct ourselves when we eat and when we earn a living. With the extra measure of holiness that Shabbat affords, "we are what we eat"—our sustenance is nothing less than "heavenly bread."

During the weekdays, reciting the blessing over a full loaf is preferable though not mandatory. Often we recite the blessing over only a partial loaf or just a single slice. This manner of eating mirrors the spiritual atmosphere of the weekdays, when we seek to mend that which has been damaged and make whole that which is deficient; when we invest so much of our energy into striving to complete what is incomplete, both in our lives and in the world at large.

In our weekday meals, even if we begin a meal reciting the blessing over a whole loaf of bread, we immediately cut off a piece, rendering the loaf incomplete. Any quality of wholeness we manage to grasp through our weekday eating generally disappears. (We can regain it only through eating in abundant holiness and reciting the Grace after Meals with intense concentration.)

On Shabbat, however, the two whole loaves of the *lechem mishneh* are a requirement. These loaves signify the aura of wholeness that Shabbat brings to the world. They reflect too the sense of completion that we ascribe to all our weekday endeavors. Beginning at sundown on Friday, and for the next twenty-five hours, we look upon the world as complete (albeit imperfect) as it is. When we recite the blessing over two whole loaves, slicing one and leaving the other intact, we envelop ourselves in wholeness, bringing an element of completeness to our Shabbat tables and to the world at large.

THE CROWN OF CREATION

Shabbat marks the completion of Creation. It is the archetype of completion, the fount from which all things derive wholeness.

We can sense this wholeness in the tranquility and harmony that Shabbat brings, in the relief of unburdening ourselves of all unfinished business. No matter how much or how little we have actually achieved during the week, if our minds are at peace with the sense that all our weekday goals have reached a level of completeness, we are in harmony with the flow of Shabbat.

(LIKUTEY HALAKHOT, SHABBAT 7:68)

The First Meal:
The Sacred Orchard

Both men and women are required
to eat three meals on Shabbat,
one at night and two during the day.

(Kitzur Shulchan Arukh #77:16)

The *Zohar* gives us the custom to begin each
of the three Shabbat meals with a salutation
acknowledging the spiritual presence
in whose honor the meal is held.
From the Ari we receive the specific formulae
of the salutation, different for each meal,
in accordance with how the presence of God,
the Holy King, is manifest at that time.
Our guest at the first Shabbat meal is
the *Shekhinah*, the "feminine face" of God,
referred to here as
the Sacred Orchard *(Chakal Tapuchin Kadishin)*.

Prepare the feast of perfect faith,
The joy of the Holy King.
Prepare the feast of the King.
This is the feast of *Chakal Tapuchin Kadishin.*
Z'er Anpin and *Atika Kadisha**
Come to feast with Her.

(BASED ON ZOHAR II, 88B)

* SEE "THE SECOND MEAL" AND "THE THIRD MEAL"

*A*ll through the week we seek our livelihood out in the "field" (see Section 2: "Lekha Dodi Hymn (1)"). With the approach of Shabbat, however, we want to separate the true source of the week's sustenance from the pull and pressure of the workplace.

To elevate the week's blessing, we recite the *Kabbalat Shabbat* at the onset of Shabbat: "Enter, O Bride...Enter, O bride, the Shabbat Queen." These feminine references serve as a welcoming to the *Shekhinah*, the feminine aspect of the Holy King, which predominates on the eve of Shabbat. All blessing and sustenance are channeled into the world through Her.

Through heeding the Creator's call to cease all creative labor with the onset of Shabbat, we acknowledge that it is God's world; through pausing our pursuit of plenty by bringing the workweek to a close, we exhibit our faith, our trust in the Holy King as the sole Provider of all our needs. This is, therefore, a preparing of "the feast of *perfect faith.*" In serving this sustenance of *emunah*, faith, at our Shabbat meals, we are sanctifying our livelihood; we are elevating the ordinary fields from which we obtain our weekly harvest into spiritual, sacred orchards.

Thus we sit down to the first meal of Shabbat after having recited the *Kabbalat Shabbat* prayer. Before partaking of the abundance we have gathered in from the "field," we recite a salutation acknowledging the *Shekhinah*—the Sacred Orchard—as the channel of our livelihood and as the spiritual presence in whose honor the nighttime meal of Shabbat is held: "*Prepare the feast of perfect faith…This is the feast of* Chakal Tapuchin Kadishin."●

UNVARYING AND EVERLASTING

The sanctity of the Festivals is facilitated by human declaration, but the sanctity of Shabbat is of a different order. Shabbat was the very first thing in Creation to be called holy—its sanctity comes directly from God.

The exalted holiness with which God invested the Shabbat is unvarying and everlasting. Its unvarying nature renders this sanctity unaffected by either human piety or human wickedness. Even if we forsake the Shabbat, her sanctity is unaffected. Its everlasting nature renders this sanctity eternal. Whenever we return to keep the Shabbat, her sanctity is on hand to show us the way.

(LIKUTEY HALAKHOT, SHABBAT 7:7)

Zemirot—
Songs:
A Simple Act
of the Heart

After eating, the Ari would sing
a Shabbat song in a pleasant voice.
He himself composed three such *zemirot,*
songs, one for each meal,
based on the hidden mysteries
associated with the holy day.

(MINHAGEI HAARI, INYANEI SHABBAT 24)

*A*pproaching God and developing a closeness to Him often begins with the simple acts: praying, good deeds, talking to God, singing and dancing. While Torah study is essential, and sharpening our intellects can take us a long way toward achieving our lofty goals, they cannot take the place of the simple devotions of the heart.

One who first embarks on the path to God may find Judaism's teachings intricate and complicated. As beginners we encounter numerous concepts in the Torah that are new and complex; the sheer breadth of the Halakhah, the corpus of Torah law and praxis that encompasses every aspect of life, can be intimidating. Achieving closeness to God can seem a daunting undertaking, a goal whose realization appears far beyond our grasp. Yet the simple acts of the heart serve as the steppingstones that can take us much further in our lifelong journey than we ever could have imagined.

Nor do these tools of simple devotion lose their effectiveness once one has become familiar with Jewish teaching. Although it is true that closeness to God hinges on the study of Torah, nevertheless, if that study is approached as nothing more than an intellectual pursuit, it contributes little if anything to one's experiencing His closeness. Knowledge of the Halakhah, too, while essential to finding the path to God, offers no guarantee that we will actually achieve our objective. If our intellectual devotions take a wrong turn or stagnate, then it is only the fuel that comes from the simple devotions of the heart that can lead us back on track.

This is the sum and substance of the *zemirot*, the special songs sung at the Shabbat table. Singing joyously from the depths of our hearts—songs of the revelation of God's Unity and of His abundant blessings, songs of our love for God and of our great delight in the Shabbat—is one of the surest ways to become close to God.

SIMPLICITY

The pure force of simplicity is essential to our realizing our potential as Jews; and few things can match the purity and the simplicity of singing at the Shabbat table. When we cast inhibition aside and sing aloud the *zemirot* of Shabbat, we discover and connect with the very essence of our Jewishness.

(LIKUTEY MOHARAN II, 104)

MARITAL RELATIONS: HOLY DELIGHTS

Marital relations are an *oneg,*
one of the physical pleasures,
associated with Shabbat.

(RAMBAM, LAWS OF SHABBAT, CHAP. 30;
SHULCHAN ARUKH, ORACH CHAIM 281:1)

Observing Shabbat has a powerful, pervasive effect on the dynamic balance of body and soul. On Shabbat, the additional flow of spiritual energy and the extra dose of joy that we experience empowers the soul. Then, more than on any other day of the week, the soul has the strength to channel the physical cravings and drives of the body. Shabbat brings to one's life a shift in favor of the soul.

The soul's ascendance on Shabbat enables the body to bring its drives, instincts and desires into perspective. Thus, taking pleasure in the various physical delights associated with Shabbat is reckoned a mitzvah; these pleasures are ordained by God, and engaging in them is the very fulfillment of His Will. Shabbat is therefore the time for festive meals, fine garments and a more restful pace. With the tempering of the body's cravings, these and the other physical pleasures of Shabbat are purged of their power to profane; indeed, they are infused with sanctity. On this day the delights of the body benefit the soul as well.

Friday night is thus an ideal time for marital relations. Although sexual cravings can be the most powerful of the body's drives, the soul, bolstered and elevated on Shabbat, is able to infuse this desire with holiness, strengthening a couple's connection with God and engendering a deep, selfless love between husband and wife. This is an essential component of marital relations and the key to the sacred unity of family.

SLEEP:
SOUL
REJUVENATION

On Shabbat morning it is customary
to begin the synagogue services
a bit later than during the week.
The reason for this custom
is that sleep is an *oneg,*
one of the physical pleasures
of Shabbat.

(KITZUR SHULCHAN ARUKH #76:10)

*E*ach night, as our bodies and minds alight into the domain of slumber, our souls slip loose from this world and ascend to the realm of the spirit. For even as sleep reduces the awareness of the mind, it paves the way for an increase in the soul's awareness. When sleep overtakes the body, the soul is renewed.

No matter how many hours one sleeps during the other nights of the week, the sleep of Shabbat has the most stirring effect in rejuvenating the soul. The seventh day possesses an inherent sanctity, and coupled with the holiness we bring to it through each of our devotions, this sanctity vanquishes the forces that would hinder the soul's advance through the spiritual realms. Our souls are quick to tap into the effusive spiritual energy that accompanies our journey through Shabbat. While our bodies enjoy the restful slumber induced by the release from the workweek that Shabbat brings, our souls reach for those realms where spiritual insight and perception are most refined.

The custom to sleep a bit longer on Shabbat morning and to begin the morning prayers in synagogue somewhat later than on the other days of the week allows our souls to bask a little longer in the exalted atmosphere of spiritual rejuvenation it finds in the sleep of Shabbat. Upon awakening, we find ourselves replenished by a fresh influx of spiritual mindfulness, one that rouses morning's declaration: "I thank You, O living and eternal King, for with compassion You have returned my soul within me."

3 | ג

SHABBAT: THE MORNING

THE MORNING:
INTRODUCTION

Our God and God of our fathers,
May You be pleased with our rest.
Sanctify us with Your mitzvahs…
Grant us Your holy Shabbat as a heritage,
And may all of Israel…rest on him.
Blessed are You, God, Who declares the Shabbat holy.

(SHABBAT MORNING PRAYER)

*T*he morning of Shabbat is a time characterized by expanding awareness. The Kabbalists tell us that the special influx of God's inspiration that descends into the world on Shabbat morning is the light of *Keter*, the Divine emanation of God's "Crown." They call this extraordinary radiance of higher spirituality "Supernal Thought," which is a metaphor for the most exalted levels of higher consciousness. This consciousness is manifest in our worldly reality as flickers of expanding awareness, as the holy thoughts and the deeper spiritual insights that can be ours on Shabbat morning.

It is only logical, then, that *Keter's* brilliance should make the morning the most uplifting and spiritually inspiring time of Shabbat. Yet many consider Friday night, with its elevating *Kabbalat Shabbat* prayer and sumptuous first Shabbat meal, to be the highest time of Shabbat. Others feel that the climax of the week is Shabbat afternoon, especially during the third meal.

Morning seems to be the time of Shabbat when people feel the least spiritually inspired. And yet the Kabbalists tell us that the higher consciousness we can awaken to on the morning of Shabbat has no equal.

Perhaps the reason we do not feel exceptionally inspired on Shabbat morning is that we lack the spiritual sensitivity necessary for assimilating *Keter's* incomparable radiance. All our sundry Shabbat preparations and the added spirituality that Friday night has introduced in our lives may be insufficient; we may still be unable to assimilate the exalted levels of God-consciousness that radiate from the highest Divine emanation. Like a crown, *Keter's* light sits on top of the head, adorning it yet remaining distinctly separate from it. Thus even on Shabbat morning when, more than at any other time during the week, Supernal Thought is within our intellectual and spiritual grasp, we perceive it as only a fleeting flash of inspiration, as a level of awareness that we can attain for a moment but cannot maintain.

Despite *Keter's* elusiveness, its radiance is so potent that it inspires us to expand our spiritual horizons. Even as a barely-sensed flicker of inspiration, the awareness that *Keter* imparts stirs us to seek deeper insight into the Torah and into the comprehensive picture of our existence. It is this element of expanding consciousness that most strongly defines the distinct atmosphere of Shabbat morning.

The ambience of Shabbat morning is enveloped in the influence of the Patriarch Avraham (as the ambiance of Friday night carries Yitzchak's influence). To this time of expanding consciousness Avraham contributes his characteristic qualities of expansiveness—a broadness and generosity that effect a reaching out to others, a stirring and quest of spirit that generate a reaching up to God. As such, Shabbat morning represents the promise of new awakenings, with Avraham's active-expansive mode of engaging the world.

We allude to this distinct atmosphere in the central blessing of the *Amidah* section of the prayer, which captures the atmosphere of each of the time frames of Shabbat.

> *Our God and God of our fathers, may You be pleased with our rest. Sanctify us with Your mitzvahs...and may all of Israel...rest on* him.

Unlike in the Friday night *Maariv* prayer, in which we refer to Shabbat as "her," in the morning *Shacharit* prayer, we refer to Shabbat in masculine terms: "may all of Israel...rest on *him*."

The Kabbalists tell us that on Shabbat morning all of us, male and female alike, receive the masculine aspect of our *neshamah yeteirah*, that extra measure of spiritual energy we gain on Shabbat. We invoke the masculine aspect of this "added soul" through the *Shacharit* and *Musaf* prayers, and through acknowledging *Atika Kadisha*, the spiritual entity corresponding to *Keter*, Whose presence graces the morning meal of Shabbat. We discern, too, undertones of the archetypal masculine in those qualities of Avraham that give Shabbat morning its particular ambiance—in the stirring for additional spiritual purity that inspires us to immerse in a mikvah a second time; in our reading from the weekly Torah portion, expounding and expanding its meaning to uncover greater coherence and awaken new meaning in our own lives; and in our reaching up to God, expanding the day of Shabbat through prayer, study and acts of kindness.

On Shabbat morning we give voice to the mode of reaching outward and upward, expanding the enlightenment we gained through Friday night's mode of looking inward. In doing so, we replace the state of receptivity with its active counterpart, at a time when expanding awareness and reaching greater levels of God-consciousness are the order of the day.

IMMERSING IN A MIKVAH:
TURNING AND RETURNING

The level of holiness on the day of Shabbat
surpasses that which preceded it on Friday night.
To benefit from this more exalted holiness,
some have the custom on Shabbat morning
to immerse again in a *mikvah*
(the special bath we immersed in on Friday
to counteract the influence of the marketplace).

(MINHAGEI HAARI, INYANEI SHABBAT 26)

*T*eshuvah is an act of penitence, a clearing of one's slate. *Teshuvah* is a turning back to God, a restoring of one's connection to Him. *Teshuvah* is purification; it is an act of self-transformation and healing. *Teshuvah* is a path to awakened awareness, to the discernment of higher levels of God-consciousness.

In all its definitions, *teshuvah* is a process.

We begin the process of *teshuvah* from the level of spiritual perception that we have at any given moment. Yet once we have succeeded to some degree to come closer to God, our perception expands. We realize then that the earlier stages of our *teshuvah*, although they may have been sincere and heartfelt, were "complete" only relative to our former level of perception; that our *teshuvah* was in fact flawed relative to our current, more refined recognition of God.

And so we set our sights on a "better *teshuvah*"—a more comprehensive repentance and a higher level of closeness, a more complete measure of healing and self-transformation. This involves a new phase of *teshuvah*—*teshuvah* over our previous, less-than-complete *teshuvah*. Guided by the stronger perception and higher awareness acquired through our earlier *teshuvah*, we feel impelled to do *teshuvah* again. We thus embark on the never-ending process of "turning and returning," each time seeking a *teshuvah* superior to that which preceded it.

The etymological root of the word *teshuvah*—*shavta*, "to return"—has the same Hebrew letters as the word *Shabbat* (שבת). Shabbat and *teshuvah*—by any definition—are conceptually one: When we delight in the Shabbat our sins are forgiven, our slates are cleared. When we abstain from our weekday work and turn away from the workaday activities that distract and distance us from God, we return to God and so restore a degree of our soul's original closeness to Him. When we pray with concentrated focus and are joyous on Shabbat, we are stirred to a more intense awareness and to higher levels of God-consciousness.

Moreover, Shabbat and *teshuvah* share certain dynamic elements. Just as the holiness of Shabbat grows in intensity with each passing hour of the day, our *teshuvah* grows with each attempt we make at turning and returning, with each increased measure of healing and spiritual awareness we introduce in our lives.

In each cycle of *teshuvah*, the earlier phases of our *teshuvah* parallel the awareness of Friday night; for both of these significant junctures signify taking the first steps toward more committed spiritual living. Subsequent phases of our *teshuvah* correspond to the higher level of awareness of Shabbat morning.

To prepare ourselves for this superior level, we immerse in the mikvah once again, for the mikvah's waters, like the act of *teshuvah*, impart a spiritual purity. Through this second, "return" immersion, in effect we are doing *teshuvah* for our preceding *teshuvah*. We emerge from the waters' depths prepared for a higher level of Shabbat awareness. ☙

LASTING TESHUVAH

Weekday *teshuvah* is born of a spontaneous impulse to realize our innate potential and achieve a greater closeness to God. It shakes us from life's comfortable numbness. Yet unless it is fanned, this initial spark of inner growth soon fades, and we return to being much the same as we were before.

Shabbat *teshuvah* is born of inner development, guided by deliberation and design. We immerse ourselves in it when the busyness of the everyday is set aside; with a mind rendered tranquil through the restfulness and repose of holiness. Shabbat *teshuvah*— even if we experience it midweek— endures and results in a lasting closeness to God.

(LIKUTEY MOHARAN I, 79)

THE
SHACHARIT
PRAYER:
A THOUSAND
BRILLIANT LIGHTS

The following blessings are inserted
into the liturgy [of the *Amidah* prayer]
… On the morning of Shabbat:
"Moshe rejoiced in the gift of his portion. . . ."

(RAMBAM, THE ORDER OF PRAYER, THE INSERTED BLESSINGS #1)

Moshe rejoiced in the gift of his portion,
   for You called him a faithful servant.
You placed a crown of beauty on his head,
   when He stood before You at Mount Sinai.
He brought down in his hand two tablets of stone,
on which were inscribed the observance of Shabbat.

*T*he Kabbalah teaches:

When Moshe ascended Mount Sinai to receive the Torah, Heaven awarded him with the radiance of a thousand brilliant lights. Later, however, when the Jewish people sinned with the Golden Calf, all but one thousandth of this radiance disappeared. Nevertheless, since Moshe himself had not transgressed, God compensated him with a lesser glow from the "crowns" with which He had graced the people at Sinai, but which He had removed from them when they sinned.

Each Shabbat, the extra measure of holiness that descends on that day causes Moshe's original, brilliant radiance to be restored. He in turn relinquishes the light of the Jewish people, which he has no desire to keep since he is content with his own light. This is indicated in the phrase "Moshe rejoiced in the gift of his portion"—the portion that has been returned to him.

Moshe has no interest in deriving personal benefit from his own righteousness; his sincere desire is that the Jewish people once again be found worthy of their light, the light manifest in the added illumination of holiness granted to each Jew who observes the Shabbat (Sha'ar HaKavanot, Kabbalat Shabbat #1).

127

These "lights" represent modes and dimensions of spiritual perception and insight. Light is a universal metaphor for consciousness: unable to comprehend something, we speak of being "in the dark" and look for ways to "bring the matter to light"; if a thought or inspiration turns on the proverbial light bulb in our heads, we say that we have been en*light*ened; an extraordinary radiance is said to emanate from the face of the wise; and wisdom, as depicted in the Book of Proverbs (4:9), is a "crown" with a magnificent glow.

Each weekday morning we don *tefillin* on our heads and on our arms next to our hearts. The leather housing of the *tefillin* and the parchments they contain act as "spiritual receptors"—making *us* more responsive to the light of consciousness. On Shabbat, however, *tefillin* are not worn, for on Shabbat we derive inspiration and heightened spiritual sensitivity from the day's unique atmosphere— through its numerous mitzvahs: the ritual laws, customs and special Shabbat prayers.

Thus in the liturgy of the Shabbat morning prayers we refer to Moshe's rejoicing over his gift of heightened consciousness and the crown of beauty that God placed on his head. In mentioning this we are reminded that we too have reason to rejoice—with the added inspiration that stirs within us the light of awareness on the Shabbat day.

READING
THE TORAH
PORTION:
THE REALITY-MAP
OF LIFE

Moshe Rabbeinu instituted
the public reading from the Torah on Shabbat
(and on Mondays and Thursdays).
Following the *Shacharit* prayer of Shabbat morning,
seven people are called up to the Torah.

(RAMBAM, LAWS OF TEFILLAH, CHAP. 12:1,15)

We struggle to understand the meaning of our lives within the broader context of our existence. Even after having committed ourselves to spiritual awareness, factoring God into all that we do, we are not always able to find significance or discover purpose in the daily occurrences and issues of our lives.

We humans live inspired—are spiritually "alive" at any given moment—only to the extent that our experience of life is meaningful, coherent and consistent with our broader understanding of things. When we can see how a specific situation or issue fits into the puzzle of life, we embrace that new element in ways that foster spiritual growth. Yet often the fit is far from obvious. The puzzle seems disjointed, its pieces mismatched; we are unable to understand their place and purpose in the larger picture. Without this understanding, we miss their meaning and coherence, and so spiritual inspiration eludes us.

God looked into the Torah and designed the world, says the Midrash (Bereishit Rabbah 1:1); thus the world was created. Far more than simply an account of the beginning and the chronicle of man, the Torah is the spiritual blueprint of the universe. Its Hebrew letters, being the elemental building blocks of holy text, are much more than mere ciphers—they are the transmitters of God's Will. As the conduits of Divine design, the Torah's letters not only depict reality; they define it. Their arrangement into words and verses bespeaks the very infrastructure of existence—everything from the macro elements of the cosmos to the microelements of the personal universes of man.

To decipher the design of his personal, individual world, man likewise looks into the Torah. Through its letters, words and verses, the Torah can be revealed as the reality-map of life. Its chapters and portions form the matrix in which each day's events and circumstances find connection and context within the larger picture of existence.

To uncover these connections and the meaning they unlock, we need to study the map—to read, analyze and interpret the Torah. It is natural for one to read the Torah through the filter of one's personal lenses. We are drawn instinctively to those elements that intrinsically reflect our individual situations and issues; the verses speak to us through the prism of the unique conditions of our lives. This is legitimate; in fact it is essential to our comprehending the puzzle of our own lives. By reading deeply those parts of the Torah that reflect our personal situations, we discover connection in the apparent disjointedness; we uncover the meaning and coherence that foster inspired spiritual growth.

The Sages divided the Scriptures, the Five Books of Torah, into weekly portions, and they divided each weekly portion into seven sections, one for each day of the week. We read the weekly portion in its entirety, however, on Shabbat morning. Each Torah portion—in the words and verses that its letters form—encompasses all the occurrences and issues that held sway over the course of the past week. By attending closely to the Torah reading on Shabbat morning, we can hear the echoes of the personal matters and individual considerations of the week gone by; we can hear too the coherence and the meaning, awakening to an awareness of their place and purpose within the comprehensive picture of our existence. ◉

Reading
the Haftarah:
Faith Masters

Following the Torah reading,
we read the *Haftarah*,
a section from a Book of Prophets
that shares some theme with
the week's Torah portion.

(Shulchan Arukh, Orach Chaim 284:1)

It once happened that the gentiles issued
a decree forbidding the study of Torah.
In place of the Torah portion,
seven people were called up to
read from a Book of Prophets. . . .
Although the decree was later rescinded,
the custom to read from the Prophets remained.

(Mishnah Berurah, ibid. :2)

*I*n every generation there are *tzaddikim*, righteous individuals, whose spiritual perception and awareness of God stem from a level of Divine inspiration. This inspiration is in certain ways akin to prophecy. Like the prophets, the *tzaddik* is a person of pure and powerful faith; and, like the prophets, he is able to strengthen the faith that others have in God.

On a Shabbat more than three thousand, three hundred years ago, God gathered the Jewish people at Mount Sinai and gave them the Torah for that very same purpose: to instill faith in the world. The Holy One handed the Tablets bearing the Ten Commandments to a human being of pure and powerful faith, instructing that *tzaddik*, Moshe *Rabbeinu* (our teacher), to disseminate the Torah's teachings and thereby strengthen others in their faith in God.

Every Shabbat down through the ages, Jews reenact the original Giving of the Torah. Gathered in the synagogue, we listen to the communal reading of the weekly portion from the Five Books of Torah and follow this with the recitation of the Haftarah. With this reading from a Book of Prophets we affirm that not only the faith of our forefathers but our infusion of faith too comes primarily through the true prophets—the *tzaddikim*—who are the masters of Divine inspiration in each generation.

Two thousands years ago, the Sages of the Talmud understood well this connection between the prophets and the Jews' faith in God. When the gentiles who ruled the Jewish people issued a decree against the study of Torah, intending to cause the Word of God to be forgotten, the Sages instituted a communal reading from a Book of Prophets. This public reading of the words of the prophets ensured that the Torah would always be remembered and—in but another form of reenacting the Giving of the Torah—strengthened the people's faith.

Nowadays, even though the gentiles' decree has long been forgotten, we retain the custom of the weekly reading of the Haftarah. We read from a Book of Prophets to show that today as well, our sole hope of fulfilling the Torah and of never forgetting its teachings hinges on our connection to the *tzaddikim* who, through their Divine inspiration and pure faith, reveal God's presence in every generation. ⬤

THE MUSAF PRAYER:
PRAYING FOR PASSION, PRAYING FOR MEANS

The time for reciting the *Musaf* prayer
begins immediately after the completion
of the morning's *Shacharit* prayer.
This parallels the *Musaf* offering
brought in the Holy Temple—
the time to bring it began immediately after
the morning *Tamid* sacrifice had been offered.

(SHULCHAN ARUKH, ORACH CHAIM 286:1;
MISHNAH BERURAH, IBID. 1)

*H*aving the motivation and desire to fulfill some mitzvah of the Torah cannot ensure that we will actually fulfill that mitzvah, if we lack the requisite means for doing so. We might *want* to improve our observance of Shabbat but may not be able to find the time for further study of its laws. We might *want* to be more charitable but may lack the temperament that makes a person giving; or we may not possess sufficient resources to enable us to share with others. If this is the case, then the sole solution is to pray—"turning Torah into prayer," as Rebbe Nachman enjoined his chassidim—by pleading with God to provide us with whatever we lack that prevents us from carrying out the mitzvah in full.

The *Musaf* prayer of Shabbat is a classic example of turning Torah into prayer. Ever since the Holy Temple in Jerusalem was destroyed some two thousand years ago, it has been impossible to fulfill physically the Torah's commandments to offer sacrifices. Instead, we discharge our obligation to bring offerings to God by *turning these commandments into prayers*; and God welcomes our entreaties in lieu of those offerings.

This is patently evident in the liturgy of the Shabbat *Musaf* prayer. We beseech God to rebuild the Temple, thereby enabling us to "perform the rites of our required offerings: the daily *Tamid* offerings in their order and the additional *Musaf* offerings in accordance with their laws." By transforming the Torah commandments associated with the *Musaf* offering into entreaties and prayers, we bring "sacrifices" to God.

Sometimes, however, we find that, indeed, we do possess the means to fulfill some mitzvah of the Torah but lack sufficient enthusiasm and passion in doing so. We are able to make time for extra Torah study, or we have adequate resources to be more charitable but are missing the inspiration that enlivens our spiritual devotions. The sole solution then is, again, to pray—*turning aspiration into prayer*. Praying for enthusiasm in carrying out any of the Torah's commandments triggers that enthusiasm. Pleading with God to provide us with the inspiration we are lacking ultimately sparks that inspiration, so that we can carry out the mitzvah *in full*. Meanwhile, our sincere entreaties to perform the mitzvah with inspiration and fervor are reckoned by God as if we had actually fulfilled it in that way. We have already drawn closer to Him. ◉

The Kedushah Declaration:
The Crown of Consciousness

The *Kedushah* (Sanctification) Hymn
recited by the congregation
when the leader repeats
the Shabbat *Musaf* prayer begins:
"Keter (a crown) is given to You,
O God our Lord."

(Zohar III:242)

*S*habbat morning is a time characterized by expanding awareness. Especially during *Musaf*-time, we have the opportunity to awaken to the special influx of God's inspiration, which shines more brightly then. This radiance of higher spirituality stems from the highest *sefirah*, *Keter*—the spiritual emanation of God's "Crown."

In the language of the *Zohar*, the light of *Keter* is called "Supernal Thought." This is a metaphor for higher consciousness—a consciousness that, throughout the week, is transcendent and so in essence beyond the landscapes of our perception, but which on Shabbat becomes immanent and thus within our intellectual and spiritual vista.

The stronger measure of spirituality that descends into the world at *Musaf*-time opens our minds to the potential for harmony in creation, to the coherence and underlying unity of all things.

We tap into this influx of higher consciousness by reciting the *Musaf* prayer and the accompanying *Kedushah*:

> A Keter *is given to You,*
>> *O God, our Lord,*
>> *by the throngs of angels on high,*
>> *together with Your people Israel assembled below.*
> *Thrice, in unison, they all declare, "Holy";*
>> *as the word spoken by Your prophet:*
>> "And they call one to the other and say,
>>> 'Holy, holy, holy is the God of Hosts;
>>> The entire world is filled with His glory.'"
> His glory *fills the universe;*
>> His *ministering angels ask one another,*
>>> "Where is the place of His glory,
>>> *that we might revere Him?"*

Heading the list of impediments to one's spiritual growth and awareness are two mistaken assumptions: the first, that one has already made the grade; the second, that one will never make the grade.

When we recite the words of the *Kedushah*—asking, "Ayeh: *Where is the place of His glory?*"—we address that part of ourselves that has made progress on the spiritual journey and that has already woken to the expanded awareness that accompanies a feeling of being close to God. In doing so, we question whether we have experienced His Presence fully, and so encourage our spiritual side to even greater accomplishment; we inform ourselves that there is still much further to go.

When we recite the words of the *Kedushah*—proclaiming, "M'lo: *The entire world is filled with His glory*"—we address that part of ourselves that has been bogged down on the spiritual journey and despaired of ever tasting the expanded awareness that accompanies a feeling of being close to God. By declaring that His Presence is found even in the everyday elements of existence, we encourage our material side to refuse to give up hope, ever; we assert that God is closer to us than we have dared to imagine.

The radiance of Supernal Thought, which shines on Shabbat morning when we recite the *Kedushah* of the *Musaf* prayer, gives scope to our awareness. Stirred by the brilliance of *Keter*, we discover the possibility of synchronizing our inner and our outer worlds. We gain a sense of the inner harmony that brings together heaven and earth, the spiritual and the corporeal—"*the throngs of angels on high, together with Your people Israel assembled below.*"

Through the increased spirituality of Shabbat morning and the unifying consciousness that it affords, we can discover the potential to integrate our higher selves with our more worldly selves, so that *"they call one to the other and say, 'Holy, holy, holy is the God of Hosts.' "* 🔵

THE
SECOND
MEAL:
A FEAST OF
CONTENTMENT
AND LIFE

The table should be set
just as for the Friday night meal. . . .
Following kiddush one washes one's hands
and recites the blessing over two whole loaves,
as at the nighttime meal.

(SHULCHAN ARUKH, ORACH CHAIM 289:1)

The custom is to begin each of the three Shabbat meals
with a salutation acknowledging the spiritual presence
in whose honor the meal is held.
The specific formula of the salutation is different for
each meal, in accordance with how the presence of God,
the Holy King, is manifest at that time.
Our guest at the second Shabbat meal is *Atika Kadisha*,
Who represents the primordial expression
of God's Supernal Will.

Prepare the feast of perfect faith, the joy of the Holy King.
Prepare the feast of the King.
This is the feast of *Atika Kadisha.*
The Sacred Orchard *(Shekhinah)* and *Z'er Anpin**
Come to feast with Him.

(BASED ON ZOHAR II, 88B)

*SEE "THE FIRST MEAL" AND "THE THIRD MEAL"

*T*here are levels of insight into the Torah that lead us to intense contemplation. These profound insights, generally beyond our intellectual and spiritual grasp, can be perceived only when a person has been truly stirred to awareness. To achieve this deep level of contemplation, Rebbe Nachman taught his chassidim, one must be fabulously wealthy and have "length of days"; qualifying that neither of these requirements is to be taken at face value.

The wealth considered necessary for intense contemplation is not the kind that is secured in a bank; even with all the riches in the world, a person is not wealthy if anxieties impoverish his spirit. Genuine wealth is an inner tranquility, born of contentment with who we are and what we have.

Neither is "length of days" to be understood in its literal sense, as long life; one can live many years and have *aged* yet never *saged.* Genuine length of days entails infusing each day with spiritual living, extending each hour of each day by filling it, through acts of holiness, with significance and value.

Both these essentials—consummate contentment and time expanded through significant, quality living—are facets of the spiritual presence known as *Atika Kadisha*, the aspect of the Holy King that predominates on the morning of Shabbat. The Kabbalists equate *Atika Kadisha* with the highest spiritual emanation, the *sefirah* of *Keter*—the "Crown," which radiates with Divine consciousness.

We return home from synagogue to partake of our meal on Shabbat morning inspired by the *Musaf* prayer, particularly by the *Kedushah* passage. With this greater spiritual sensitivity comes the opportunity to open our minds to the radiance of *Keter*. Although this higher consciousness emanating from *Atika Kadisha* is beyond our ability to integrate and maintain, it is the source of the profound Torah insights that we perceive when, filled with the spirit of Shabbat, we grow rich with contentment and expand the day through our prayers, study and acts of kindness.

Thus when we sit down to the second Shabbat meal we recite a salutation acknowledging *Atika Kadisha* as the channel through which we are stirred to higher consciousness and as the spiritual presence in whose honor the morning meal of Shabbat is held: *"Prepare the feast of perfect faith…This is the feast of* Atika Kadisha.*"*

SHABBAT EATING

We eat the Shabbat meals not to gratify ourselves or to satiate our appetites, but to open the channels of blessing that Shabbat draws into the other days of the week.

(LIKUTEY MOHARAN I, 276)

4 | ד

SHABBAT:
THE
AFTERNOON

The Afternoon:
Introduction

Our God and God of our fathers,
May You be pleased with our rest.
Sanctify us with Your mitzvahs…
Grant us Your holy Shabbat as a heritage,
And may all of Israel…rest on them.
Blessed are You, God, Who declares the Shabbat holy.

(Shabbat Afternoon Prayer)

*T*he afternoon is upon us. The sun's light that filled the sky is now on the wane.

The Kabbalah teaches that in the beginning, God's Infinite Light filled all of existence. There were neither created beings nor anything that could be characterized as space, emptiness or void. Therefore when the E*in* S*of*, the Infinite One, wanted to create the world, there was nowhere to create it. To make a place for the universe, God contracted His Infinite Light, leaving an empty space for spirit and matter to come into existence.

The masters of Kabbalah termed this primordial act of Divine contraction *tzimtzum* ("constriction"), but they cautioned us not to take this concept literally, for it is impossible to apply a spatial model to God. One conceptual rendering of the principle of *tzimtzum* relates it to human participation in the process of creation of the world.

Prior to the world's creation, all that existed was God's infinite wholeness and perfection. Had God created the world perfect and whole, as a simple extension of His Being, incompleteness would not have existed. Through the primordial act of *tzimtzum*, God, the E*in* S*of*, contracted and concealed His perfection, and in so doing, created the concept of imperfection and deficiency. He thus left unfinished work in the world; the creative process wanted completing. This is the impetus for all human endeavor and accomplishment. Human beings were created to be God's "partners" in Creation (see insert, next page).

While the *tzimtzum* was an essential catalyst for Creation, it also gave rise to the concept of *dinim*, "judgments": concealment of God's perfection introduced into the creation the potential for adversity and suffering—the various means through which Heaven's abundant goodness is hidden from the world.

"On the seventh day God *finished* the work that He had been doing...God blessed the seventh day...because on it He *abstained* from all the work that He had *created to do*" (Genesis 2:3).

Which is it? asks the Midrash *(Bereishit Rabbah 11:7* and *Rashi)*: Did God "finish the work" as the beginning of the verse indicates, or, did He "abstain from all the work" that was still to be done? Was the world complete, or was it left incomplete?

In fact the Creator did finish the work He was intending to do. What God left unfinished was the work He "created *for human beings* to do."

God could have made a world free of disease and poverty, a world in which we do not have to toil for a living or struggle to make ourselves better human beings. But the Divine plan was to make us His partners in the creative process. He "abstained from all *this* work" and left us to complete the unfinished work of Creation.

As we endeavor to claim our place as God's partners in Creation, we experience these judgments as the obstacles that thwart our efforts to perfect the world. We experience judgments in our daily lives in the form of the difficulties and frustrations we encounter in negotiating our everyday existence; as the limitations that inhibit personal growth; and as the barriers that keep us distant from God. On the cosmic level, *dinim*—judgments—are the forces of fragmentation that impede Supernal Unity, hence they are the barriers that keep God's bounteous good from reaching us.

The process of *tzimtzum* takes place again and again, day after day. Throughout the week, the waning of the sun's light each afternoon parallels the daily contracting of the Infinite Light. Each day God contracts His Light during Minchah-time, leaving an "empty space" in which to create tomorrow's new day. He conceals His perfection, allowing for incompleteness and deficiency—the very factors that beget tomorrow's new challenges. And in the dynamic, the Minchah-time *dinim* are awakened.

The exception to this daily process is the afternoon of Shabbat, the spiritual climax of the week. Although during the week the afternoon is marked by powerful judgments, on Shabbat the exalted holiness of the day transforms Minchah-time into a time of great Divine favor. The influx of abundant grace that fills the world on Shabbat counteracts the *dinim*; all of creation moves one step closer to perfection.

The Supernal oneness in the cosmic realm that prevails then is mirrored in hints of harmony and wholeness that beckon to us in the personal realm. With the *dinim* eliminated, the notion of tackling the unfinished work of the world appears less daunting; our personal and spiritual goals seem within the realm of the possible. It is the time to unite the enlightenment we gained through Friday's receptive mode with the expanding awareness of Shabbat morning's active mode; we assimilate Yitzchak's qualities with those of Avraham, creating a harmonious and unified whole.

The characteristic qualities of the Patriarch Yaakov define the aura of Shabbat afternoon (as Yitzchak's qualities define the aura of Friday night and Avraham's qualities define the aura of Shabbat morning). To this time of oneness and unity Yaakov imparts his compelling influence of balance, harmony, and wholeness achieved through integration.

We allude to this distinct ambiance (as we did on Friday night and Shabbat morning) in the central blessing of the *Amidah* prayer.

> *Our God and God of our fathers, may You be pleased with our rest. Sanctify us with Your mitzvahs...and may all of Israel...rest on* them.

In contrast to the *Maariv* prayer, where we refer to Shabbat using a feminine pronoun, and unlike the *Shacharit* prayer, where we refer to Shabbat using a masculine pronoun, in the *Minchah*, afternoon prayer, we use the plural construction: "...may all of Israel...rest on *them*."

On the afternoon of Shabbat, the two sides of our *neshamah yeteirah* (the extra measure of spiritual energy we gain on Shabbat)—the feminine aspect we receive on Friday night and the masculine aspect we receive on Shabbat morning—come together in a harmonious whole of the feminine-masculine totality. We invoke this oneness through the liturgy of the *Minchah* prayer and through welcoming *Z'er Anpin*, the spiritual archetype of integration, Whose presence graces the afternoon meal of Shabbat.

We can sense this archetypal oneness through those qualities of Yaakov that give Shabbat *Minchah*-time its unique ambiance, particularly when we involve ourselves in the study of a Torah lesson of the *tzaddik* at the third Shabbat meal. With the *dinim* banished, we are able to open ourselves to this righteous teacher's words with heightened receptivity. We are then best attuned to discover the expanding awareness that they cultivate. In this integrative mode that reveals the oneness in all of life, we can best internalize the higher consciousness embodied in the *tzaddik's* teaching. To the extent that we succeed in integrating this consciousness, we can find our way to wholeness. In the oneness that characterizes *Minchah*-time of Shabbat, this God-consciousness brings us closer to becoming the complete human beings we were born to be. 🕎

GOD'S INFINITE LIGHT

The more distracted we are by the static interference created by everyday living, the more God clothes His Infinite Light in "garments" of corporeality in order for us to perceive it. Thus the less we in fact perceive of the Light's genuine illumination.

But on Shabbat God reveals His Infinite Light by clothing it only in the diaphanous garments of spirituality. We detect it not through *melakhah*–work and everyday activity, but through Shabbat's ritual laws and customs and through the serenity unique to the day of rest. Thus the more we in fact perceive of the illumination of God's Light.

(LIKUTEY HALAKHOT, TECHUMIN 4:25)

THE MINCHAH PRAYER:
IN THE ONENESS
OF ETERNITY

The following blessings are inserted
into the liturgy [of the *Amidah* prayer]
…on the afternoon of Shabbat:
"You are One and Your Name is One…
a perfect *menuchah,* rest, in which You find favor."

(RAMBAM, THE ORDER OF PRAYER, THE INSERTED BLESSINGS #1)

You are One and Your Name is One;
and who is like Your people Israel, one nation on earth?
A splendor of greatness and a crown of salvation
is the day of respite and holiness
that You have given to Your people...
Yaakov and his children rest on it:
a loving and generous *menuchah,*
a true and genuine *menuchah,*
a *menuchah* of peace and tranquility,
of stillness and security,
a perfect *menuchah* in which You find favor.

L ong before social scientists abandoned uniformity as a model for social integration, before anyone replaced melting pot with mosaic, the Torah identified diversity as the essential seedbed of true harmony and peace. It is out of our distinctions, not out of our sameness, that genuine unity and oneness blossom.

Nevertheless, one might assume the very opposite to be true: that to ensure greater harmony and peace we need to be alike—as identical as possible in our interests and attitudes, as similar as we can be in our tastes and priorities. Indeed, there are those who would argue that this is a basic goal of religion. The truth, however, is that sameness is not at all what our Creator intends for humanity.

God created every individual as a unique expression of the Infinite. He instilled each of us with a singular mind-set and a distinctive array of capabilities, intending that we each actualize that uniqueness to the fullest while learning to recognize the fundamental connectedness of all things. Thus, hardwired into the reality of His creation is the immutable principle that *the greatest unity emerges from diversity*, when people of different minds learn to accept one another—recognizing and respecting the different and living in harmony.

God's partiality for a unity born of diversity is manifest in numerous facets of life, not the least of which is Jewish law. In cases of halakhic dispute, when there are diverse opinions regarding how to rule, the Torah instructs us to follow the majority. This principle does not stem from the notion that might makes right, nor even from the logical conclusion that the majority opinion carries greater intellectual weight. The reason God favors the majority opinion over that of the individual or of the minority is that it is a greater expression of unity and respect for others.

The Talmud states that just as no two people look exactly alike, neither can two people be found who think exactly alike. No two individuals will view a matter in precisely the same way or draw the identical conclusions from what they have seen. The opinion of the majority is therefore the opinion that *individuals* share. What God finds so very pleasing is that, despite their different personal viewpoints and perspectives, all these individuals have articulated a single, unified opinion and, as one, have *agreed to it*.

This exquisite formulation of a unified halakhic opinion of individuals finds its parallel in the cosmic essence of the character of Shabbat afternoon. As the sun turns westward to vanish below the horizon on Shabbat, each of the individual days of the preceding week are joined in the oneness of this hour of spiritual climax. Like the seven different colors of the rainbow which, when combined, return to the whiteness that begot them, so each of the week's separate days—bearing all their diversity—return to their source in the oneness of eternity that characterizes the interlude of Minchah-time on Shabbat.

It is to this eternal oneness that we refer in the Minchah prayer, and thus the concept of "perfect menuchah" is defined: it is the oneness of God and the Jewish people—the oneness we can experience in the "peace, tranquility, stillness and security" of Shabbat afternoon. We pray for a unity hewed of diversity—for all of Sunday and Monday and Tuesday...to unite in the "day of respite and holiness"—and by praying in this way, to contribute consciously to its happening, on both the cosmic and the personal level. ☙

A SIMPLE UNITY

Our world changes at a dizzying speed, turning yesterday's certainties into today's uncertainties, and today's uncertainties into tomorrow's apprehensions and concerns. Seemingly random and meaningless events are redesigning the reality of our lives constantly.

In the illuminating inspiration of Minchah-time of Shabbat we discover that through the bewildering multiplicity of creation shines the simple unity of One Creator. Our rapidly shifting realities, far from being meaningless or random, are the purposeful design of the Divine Will. This awareness allays our apprehension. The world, rather than being the center of confusion and darkness, becomes a stage for the unfolding of God's Infinite Light.

(LIKUTEY MOHARAN II, 2:6)

Reading From the Torah: Spiritual Training

At *Minchah*...a Torah scroll
is taken out of the Ark.
Three people are called up,
and [some] ten verses are read
from the Torah portion of
the coming Shabbat.

(Shulchan Arukh, Orach Chaim 292:1)

*T*HE FIRST RULE OF SPIRITUAL GROWTH: *The way up begins with the way down —never despair!*

Along the journey that takes us closer to God we must never give up hope. After each setback—each time the goal we have set for ourselves eludes us, each time our deeds fail to coincide with our principles and ideals—we must be willing to try again. This resolve and determination to "keep on keeping on" are essential to our eventual realization of our spiritual aspirations.

THE SECOND RULE OF SPIRITUAL GROWTH: *Every effort counts! Every good intention and desire makes a difference!*

The doggedness that will enable us to turn our backs on despair, and the tenacity we need to stay the course, hinge on our recognizing that none of our spiritual strivings, however meager, are ever wasted or lost. Though we may feel ourselves starting over from scratch, again and again, all our efforts are in fact cumulative. Each of our attempts builds up our spiritual brawn.

These are the messages we take from the week's three abridged Torah readings. Before we read the weekly Torah portion in full on Shabbat morning in synagogue, we read its first ten or so verses at *Minchah*-time of the preceding Shabbat, and again on Monday morning and Thursday morning of the preceding week.

Completing the Torah portion is our spiritual goal. Beginning the week's portion on three separate occasions, each time without completing it, helps us internalize the two very important principles that tell us *never to despair* and that *all our efforts and intentions count.*

Like the three abbreviated Torah readings, all our beginnings—all our many false starts and frustrated attempts —are indispensable. It is the spiritual training we get from starting over and over again that enables us eventually to complete our spiritual journey, from beginning to end.

THE THIRD MEAL:
THE "ALEPH"
OF WHOLENESS

One must be very scrupulous about
conducting the third meal of Shabbat. . . .
The time for holding the third meal
begins at *Minchah*-time.

(SHULCHAN ARUKH, ORACH CHAIM 291:1,2)

The custom is to begin each of the three Shabbat meals
with a salutation acknowledging the spiritual presence
in whose honor the meal is held.
The specific formula of the salutation is different for
each meal, in accordance with how the presence of God,
the Holy King, is manifest at that time.
Our guest at the third Shabbat meal is *Z'er Anpin,*
Who represents the channel of Divine Providence—
encompassing both God's actions toward human beings
and His responses to human actions.

Prepare the feast of perfect faith, the joy of the Holy King.
Prepare the feast of the King.
This is the feast of *Z'er Anpin*.
Atika Kadisha and the *Shekhinah* (the Sacred Orchard)*
Come to feast with Him.

(BASED ON ZOHAR II, 88B)

* SEE "THE SECOND MEAL" AND "THE FIRST MEAL"

*A*leph is the first letter of the word *adam*, human being. The first letter of a Hebrew word is the most significant, for it encapsulates the essence of what the word represents.

With directed perception, we could see in the *aleph* of *adam* the essence of a human being. We could follow, through the form of the *aleph*, the whole of the human spiritual trek: from the initial diminishing of worldly attachment to the stirrings of wakefulness to the wholeness that comes through integrating the spiritual.

The form of the letter *aleph* (א) is comprised of three distinct components: two dots and a line, represented in Hebrew letters as two *yuds* (י) and a *vav* (ו). Each of the three parts of the *aleph* corresponds to one of the three Shabbat meals.

The first *yud*, the one to the left of the *vav* and below it, alludes to a state of lower consciousness. This is the level of human awareness at the first stages of the spiritual quest, as one struggles to break free of one's worldly pursuits and to elevate the sparks of holiness (see Section 1: "Refraining from Creative Labor"). The lower *yud* thus corresponds to the eve of Shabbat, when we separate ourselves from the workweek and elevate our blessings from the field. This is the time of the first meal of Shabbat, the feast of the Sacred Orchard.

The second *yud*, to the right of the *vav* and above it, alludes to a state of higher consciousness. This is the level of human awareness at the more advanced stages of the quest, after one has disengaged from one's attachments to the worldly and has immersed oneself in the pursuit of God-consciousness. The upper *yud* thus corresponds to the morning of Shabbat, when we are stirred to a higher consciousness, a level that is yet beyond our ability to integrate. This is the time of the second meal of Shabbat, the feast of *Atika Kadisha*.

The two *yuds* are linked by a *vav*. As its shape and position implies, the *vav* is a bridge between the higher and the lower; it is the channel that enables higher consciousness to flow from above to below. By uniting the upper *yud* with the lower *yud*, the *vav* completes the *aleph*, making *adam* whole. Through the essence of the *vav*, we can internalize the Divine consciousness emanating from *Atika Kadisha*, the higher influence that makes its presence felt on the morning of Shabbat.

We approach wholeness only to the degree that we succeed in bridging heaven and earth, opening a channel to enable the flow of Divine consciousness. Once we are stirred to that higher consciousness and have begun to internalize and incorporate it within ourselves, we can become the complete human beings we were born to be.

Our spiritual quest for wholeness reaches its peak each week on Shabbat at *Minchah*-time. The oneness and unity manifest then in the cosmic realm are reflected in our successfully integrating higher consciousness. This integration is a feature of *Z'er Anpin*, the aspect of the Holy King that predominates on the afternoon of Shabbat. Like the *vav* that joins the higher realms to the lower, *Z'er Anpin* is the primary facet of the Holy King through which God and human beings interact. At *Minchah*-time on Shabbat, the interaction facilitated by the influence of *Z'er Anpin* is at its strongest.

Thus when we sit down to the third Shabbat meal we recite a salutation acknowledging *Z'er Anpin* as the channel for our wholeness and as the spiritual presence in whose honor the afternoon meal of Shabbat is held: *"Prepare the feast of perfect faith...This is the feast of Z'er Anpin."*

A Torah
Lesson:
Soul Desire

Many have the custom to eat
the third meal of Shabbat
in the synagogue as a communal meal.
The *tzaddikim,* righteous individuals
accomplished in Torah,
traditionally deliver a lesson then.

(Likutey Maharei'akh 2, Seudah Shlishit)

"You shall proclaim the Shabbat an *oneg* (delight),"
says the prophet (Isaiah 58:13).
What constitutes "a delight"?
It is as the Sages taught:
One should prepare the most delicious
foods and drinks for one's Shabbat meals.

(Rambam, Laws of Shabbat, chap. 30:1,7)

*A*mong the most powerful of all spiritual experiences is the one that can be ours during the time we spend eating. This experience—a boundless, unfathomable yearning of the soul for God—is known as the illumination of Desire. The Kabbalists explain that Desire, another name for Divine Will, is the élan vital of the universe. God willed the world into existence, and His Will is the life force that continues to sustain and energize the universe to this very moment.

Human will, being a spark of the Divine Will, serves a similar purpose. Our will sustains us; our wants, longings and desires together constitute the essential driving force behind all we do. And of the sundry ways in which we boost the level of our energy and life force, eating is the most basic and direct. Nevertheless, it is also one of the trickiest and most fraught with danger.

The food we eat sustains and enlivens us. We can use this vitality to intensify our material and physical pleasure—satisfying the body's will and desire; or, alternatively, we can use that same vitality to intensify our closeness to God—fulfilling the soul's ultimate will and desire. The more a person uses the energy and life force that he acquires through eating to champion the soul's will, the stronger grows the illumination of his soul's desire.

> After Rabbi Shimon bar Yochai would complete the third meal of Shabbat, a voice from heaven would proclaim: "Then you will delight over God..." (Zohar II, 88b).

The *Zohar* teaches that the sustenance gained from the food we eat on Shabbat is entirely spiritual; the Shabbat meals fortify the will of the soul and foster—even in the body—a desire to assist the soul in achieving its goal.

This is the reason the Torah instructs us to "proclaim the Shabbat *a delight*." O*neg*, the Hebrew term for "delight," is comprised of the letters *ayin* (ע), *nun* (נ) and *gimel* (ג). The *ayin* stands for A*yden*, Eden; the *nun* stands for *nahar*, a river; the *gimel* stands for *gan*, a garden. O*neg*, delight, is thus an allusion to the verse from Genesis (2:10) that depicts the earliest stages of Creation: "A *river* issues from E*den* to water the G*arden*." The *oneg* we experience from eating the Shabbat meals is thus nothing less than the life force of the universe—the river—which issues from the fount of Divine Will—Eden—and fills the heart—the Garden.

This surge of life force, the spiritual sustenance that nourishes the soul and intensifies its desire for God, is strongest during the third meal of Shabbat, when the three elements of *oneg* are complete—when the *river* from E*den* flows into and waters the G*arden*.

Thus at the third meal of Shabbat—when the potential for integrating higher consciousness is greatest, when the soul's longing to be filled with a boundless yearning for God is strongest—the *tzaddik* teaches a Torah lesson. In the oneness of eternity that characterizes M*inchah*-time on Shabbat, the *tzaddik's* teaching links the souls of those present to Divine Will and transforms the delight of Shabbat that fills their hearts into an illumination of Desire. ●

THE HUB OF THE WEEK

Our tradition presents the centrality of Shabbat in the week in two separate modes: As the culmination of the six days of Creation, Shabbat is the essence of completion and completeness; it concludes the progression of the six days of the week.

Alternately, Shabbat is central, like the hub of a wheel that has six spokes. It is the heart of the week, the nucleus from which each day draws its spiritual energy. Without Shabbat, the wheel of life could not turn.

(LIKUTEY MOHARAN II, 39)

ה|5

SHABBAT: ON THE WAY OUT

On the
Way Out:
Introduction

 שבת

On Friday evening
God gives a person a *neshamah yeteirah,*
an extra measure of spiritual energy,
and on Saturday night
He takes it away.

(BEITZA 16)

On Saturday night, the holiness of Shabbat begins to fade away. With it, the *neshamah yeteirah*—that extraordinary measure of spiritual sensitivity that first appears with the cessation of work on Friday night, and then develops and becomes whole over the course of the Shabbat—begins to withdraw as well.

While we cannot prevent the departure of the *neshamah yeteirah*, our longing for it enables us to retain a modicum of its light. If we lament the loss of the "added soul," the additional spiritual energy we gain on Shabbat, and yearn for the heightened sensitivity that brings us closer to God, we can keep a spark of the *neshamah yeteirah* glowing throughout the week. For the secret to soul-making is in the longing and the yearning.

This is the lesson Rebbe Nachman taught his followers in connection with the Talmud's reading of "shavat vayinafash," arranging the words to read *shavat vay nefesh* (see insert). On a more basic level, the Talmud relates the declaration of

How do we know that a person is given a *neshamah yeteirah* on Friday evening? The Sages of the Talmud *(Beitza 16a)* derive this from the verse that states that on Shabbat God ceased and rested from the work of creating heaven and earth *(see* Exodus 31:17). The double language, *"shavat vayinafash* (ceased and rested)," suggests that on Shabbat, when, like God, we human beings too bring an end to our weekday "creating," we have two souls that enjoy the respite: our regular soul, and the extra soul that each of us receives on the holiest day of the week.

How do we know that the *neshamah yeteirah* is taken away from us on Saturday night? The Sages deduce this by reading the words *"shavat vayinafash"* as *"shavat vay nefesh"*—as soon as Shabbat ceases *(shavat)* and comes to an end, woe *(vay)*, for the soul *(nefesh)* departs.

these words to the end of Shabbat, but on a deeper level, Rebbe Nachman relates them to the departure of the *neshamah yeteirah*, as we proclaim at the onset of Shabbat, "Woe, for the soul will depart on Saturday night." On Friday afternoon, the *neshamah yeteirah* has yet to arrive, yet we lament its anticipated loss then. By longing for the heightened spiritual sensitivity that will inevitably depart, we actually bring the *neshamah yeteirah* into existence.

The almost tangible energy created by our longing, which allows the *neshamah yeteirah* to take hold, also enables us to hold onto it throughout the week. The essence of this *neshamah* departs on Saturday night, yet through our yearning we can keep its afterglow kindled.

Our objective on Saturday night is to infuse the physical dimension with spirit, to imprint our workaday consciousness with Shabbat consciousness. The inspiration we carry away from Shabbat fuels us in the week ahead. The higher awareness enables us to focus throughout the week on life's subtler, spiritual aspects; through it we learn to moderate the demands and pressures of the material world that rule our lives and impinge on our freedom.

Our longing extends the glow of the *neshamah yeterirah* beyond the boundaries of Shabbat, and the mitzvahs—the laws, customs and liturgy—of Saturday night extend the higher God-consciousness we gain on the seventh day into the everyday of our lives.

On Saturday night, the workaday mentality, which we set out to vanquish at the onset of Shabbat, begins to resurface. It is time to begin again to stave off the allures of the marketplace and the obstacles it places in the way of spiritual living. By means of the liturgy of the *Maariv* prayer of Saturday night, we infuse our weekdays with

Shabbat awareness and with the protection it affords us throughout the week.

Through the *Havdalah* ceremony as well, we inject the spiritual fuel of Shabbat consciousness into the week. This is highly evident in the *Havdalah* blessing, in which we distinguish the sacred from the secular, the seventh day from the six days of the week. This discrimination, though it underscores the *differences* between the holy and the mundane, is the conduit for imparting the sanctity and higher awareness of Shabbat to the weekdays. The other elements of the *Havdalah* ceremony too—the blessings over wine, fragrance and fire—are designed to carry over to the week the spiritual rectifications that Shabbat affords.

And this is likewise the reason for *Melaveh Malka*, the meal we eat to escort the departing Shabbat Queen. Being both the "fourth" meal of Shabbat and the first meal of the new week, *Melaveh Malka* shares in the sacred and in the secular and can thus transform our eating into a conscious act of the mind and soul. It accommodates our applying the higher levels of Shabbat consciousness to our day-to-day lives. Hence the spiritual presence of King David graces the meal of Saturday night; it is his characteristic quality—sanctifying the mundane—that gives *Melaveh Malka*, and indeed all of Saturday night, its distinct character and tone. ⬤

THE
MAARIV
PRAYER:
SHELTER FROM
THE STORM

The *Maariv* prayer following Shabbat
is recited somewhat later than usual,
so that the holiness of Shabbat
embraces the weekdays.

(SHULCHAN ARUKH, ORACH CHAIM 293:1)

During the weekdays,
the *Hashkiveinu* passage of the *Maariv* prayer
concludes with the words:
"May He watch over His people Israel forever."

(TUR, ORACH CHAIM 236)

Our efforts to build spiritual lives often fall prey to the everyday aspects and activities of life, particularly to that most everyday activity of earning a livelihood. We'd like to inject some spiritual sense or meaning into our job or profession, but the allures of career and fortune get in the way, clouding our spiritual vision; we set our sights on maintaining a high moral standard in all our business dealings but find ourselves repeatedly sacrificing our principles on the altar of self-indulgence and monetary gain. The pressures that sidetrack our noble goals again and again create countless potholes in the road that heads toward spiritual successes in day-to-day endeavors.

These obstacles assault us throughout the week, when we need an extra measure of protection to shield us from the enticements that would bait us away from spiritual living. This is why we conclude the *Hashkiveinu* passage of the weekday *Maariv* prayer with the request, "May [God] watch over His people Israel forever."

On Shabbat, however, our spiritual quest stands a far better chance of proceeding according to plan. Our Shabbat devotions and prayers, and the greater awareness they bring, weaken the allures of the marketplace, diminishing their influence over us. We make our way through Shabbat without the need for extra protection; indeed, there is no more effective shield to ward off the impediments to leading a spiritual life than the encompassing holiness of the day. This is why on Shabbat, instead of concluding the *Hashkiveinu* passage with a request that God watch over His people, we close it with the declaration, "Blessed are You, God, Who spreads the *sukkah* (tent) of peace over us."

The *sukkah*, the Sages tell us, symbolizes the Clouds of Glory, which surrounded the Jewish people on all sides when they journeyed through the wilderness. These Clouds straightened the rough spots along the way, smoothing the people's path and protecting them from harm. When we declare that God spreads His "*sukkah* of peace," we are affirming the superior protection from the impediments to spirituality that Shabbat brings—the security and tranquility that come only when we are enveloped in the all-encompassing shelter of God.

But when the holy day departs, the workaday mentality and the accompanying attraction and obstacles of the marketplace reappear. At night, therefore, as soon as Shabbat ends, we return to the weekday *Maariv* liturgy, again praying for God's protection in the *Hashkiveinu* passage. This prayer, which concludes with the request that God watch over us, also includes a request that God "spread the *sukkah* of peace over us." Thus in the weekday *Maariv* we petition God for the special, superior shelter of Shabbat. We recognize that even during the week God's protection, which bolsters our spiritual quest, is drawn from Shabbat—from its holiness and from the awareness we gain on the seventh day.

Extending the awareness of the seventh day into our everyday lives entails giving Shabbat a prominent place in our activities as we engage in the pursuit of our livelihood, bearing in mind that the money we earn during the week will enable us to purchase sumptuous foods, fine clothing and other things to enhance the honor of the Shabbat. In this way we infuse the weekdays with a higher awareness of the seventh day—with the protection of God's "*sukkah* of peace." This Shabbat awareness throughout the week protects us from the enticements of the workaday mentality and the tendency to forfeit our principles for the sake of material gain.

On another level, our weekday awareness of Shabbat rouses us to the higher values in life: to giving charity with the money we earn, and to making Torah study and spiritual pursuits a high priority in the routines of our lives; and it instills in us trust in God—with the recognition that we gain our livelihood by means of the intelligence, the faculties and the means that He alone provides.

The Havdalah Ceremony (1): Distinguishing the Difference

The *Havdalah* blessing is recited,
once in the *Amidah* prayer of *Maariv*,
in the blessing of
"You endow man with knowledge and
teach discernment to humankind...,"
and once again, over a cup of wine.

(Shulchan Arukh, Orach Chaim 294:1)

Blessed are You, God...
Who separates between the sacred and the mundane,
between the light and the darkness...
between the seventh day and the six days of the week.

(THE HAVDALAH BLESSING)

*I*n the beginning, when "the earth was yet unformed and empty, with darkness over the face of the deep" (Genesis 1:1), God created *hierarchy*. He thus replaced chaos with order: He set the earth below and heaven above; He placed an expanse of sky in the midst of the waters to separate the upper waters from the lower waters; He fashioned a greater light to preside over the day and a lesser light to preside over the night.

When "God then blessed the seventh day and declared it holy" (Genesis 2:1-3), He created a hierarchy of days, designating Shabbat as primary and all the rest as secondary. Creation—as the introduction of a hierarchical code—was thus complete; to bring an egalitarian rejection of hierarchy into this scheme of the universe would throw the creation back into chaos.

Shabbat is the essence of creation, the root of all that is holy. The rest of the week has purpose solely within the context of its relationship to the seventh day. Yet unless we ourselves recognize the primary place Shabbat holds in creation—unless we discriminate between the holiness of Shabbat and the mundanity of the weekdays—it is easy to mistake Shabbat for just another day. For what perceptible difference is there, after all, between one day and another?

Only God's introducing a hierarchical system into a universe "yet unformed and empty" replaced chaos with organization and order. Only our discernment of the hierarchy—primary and secondary, Shabbat and the weekdays—spares us from the chaos and emptiness of one day running into another.

Reciting the *Havdalah* blessing at the close of Shabbat instills this recognition in ourselves. Through the *Havdalah* ceremony we distinguish the sacred from the secular, the seventh day from the six days of the week. Paradoxically, this discrimination, which underscores the essential *absence* of holiness during the week, is the bridge that imparts sanctity to the mundane; it is this that carries the holiness of Shabbat over to the weekdays. These six days are rectified and elevated predominantly by means of the efforts we invest during the week for the sake of Shabbat. The first of these weekday efforts for Shabbat is our recitation of *Havdalah*—introducing hierarchy to a week that is "yet unformed and empty."

◆

The *Havdalah* (literally, "separation") ceremony constitutes an essential distinguishing between "the sacred and the mundane…between the seventh day and the six days of the week." In making these distinctions we are discerning between two truths: the higher, perfect truth that peeks through on Shabbat, and the partial truth that dominates the weekdays (see Section 2: "Candle Lighting").

The truth of Shabbat is a truth pristine and absolute—truth as it was prior to the six days of Creation. The truth of the weekdays, on the other hand, is an altogether different semblance of truth—truth as it has been ever since the time of Creation. For concurrent with the creation of the world there came into existence the first traces of a lesser truth, a relative truth. This was the inevitable byproduct of the emerging reality of our universe, a dualistic reality in which a multitude of created beings live their lives ostensibly separate from God. This first falsehood of seeming separation from God engendered a weekday truth—a truth that begs to be distinguished from and refined of the falsehood in which it is entangled.

Once this second truth emerged in the cosmic realm—an amalgamated truth embodied within the Tree of Knowledge of Good and Evil—it was not long before it became part of everyday human reality. The moment Adam ate from the forbidden fruit of the Tree, the first human reinforced the commingling of truth and falsehood, internalizing it as an integral component of his consciousness. Truth, once apparent and absolute, became clouded and partial. Distinctions, once evident and unequivocal, became relative and mired in ambiguity. Sacred and secular are thus barely distinguishable.

In reciting the *Havdalah* we distinguish between two levels of truth. We note the difference between the weekday truth, which emerged during the six days of Creation, and the truth of the reality that existed prior to Creation. It is this second truth that we come to know through our observance of Shabbat. At the core of this awareness that *Havdalah* affords is the recognition that there *is* a difference—a very great difference—the mundane is less complete than the sacred, the darkness less than the light, the weekdays less than Shabbat. When we make this awareness a part of our everyday reality, we infuse the weekdays of our lives with priceless morsels of hierarchy, higher truth and holiness. ☙

The Havdalah Ceremony (2): At the Center of Creation

The order of the *Havdalah* ceremony through
which we bid Shabbat farewell is as follows:
One recites the blessings over wine,
then over fragrance and [the illumination of
the fire of a multi-wicked] candle,
and finally one recites the *Havdalah* blessing.

(Shulchan Arukh, Orach Chaim 296:1)

*A*t night, as Shabbat departs, we reexperience several of the motifs we encountered at the onset of Shabbat. When we first greeted the Shabbat Queen we recited blessings over the candles, over fragrance and, in the kiddush, over a cup of wine. We bid her farewell in much the same way, by reciting the blessings of the *Havdalah* ceremony over wine, fragrance and the illumination of a multi-wicked candle.

Not only the themes but also the liturgy of each of these two ceremonies are parallel. In the kiddush we bear witness to the superior sanctity of Shabbat by reciting the *Vayechulu* passage, proclaiming that God brought the world into existence during the six days of Creation but on the seventh day ceased His work and declared the Shabbat holy. And in the *Havdalah* blessing we proclaim that God "separates between the sacred and the mundane, between the light and the darkness...between the seventh day and the six days of the week."

These parallels in praxis and liturgy disclose the common primary purpose of greeting the Shabbat as she arrives and bidding her farewell as she departs: to infuse the weekdays with the sanctity of the seventh day. We can discern their relationship more clearly if, instead of thinking of Shabbat as the *end* of the week, we consider its centrality in creation as reflected in its position in the order of the days. Actually, Shabbat is the *middle* of the week—following days four, five and six, and preceding days one, two and three. The mitzvahs of the onset of Shabbat are retroactive, illuminating the three weekdays just passed. The parallel mitzvahs we perform immediately after Shabbat are anticipatory, illuminating the three weekdays just ahead. Their purpose—to bring spiritual rectification (*tikkun*) to the weekdays—is the same.

◆

HAVDALAH WINE

According to one opinion in the Midrash, the fruit of the
Tree of Knowledge of Good and Evil from which Adam and
Eve tasted was actually the grape. This accounts for the
dual nature of wine; it has the capacity to awaken a
longing for closeness to God—the knowledge of good—
but it also has the capacity to dull all spiritual sensitivity
and aspiration—the knowledge of evil.

The weekdays, too, are of a dual nature; like wine, they
are identified with the Tree of Knowledge. By reciting the
kiddush over a cup of wine at the onset of Shabbat, not
only do we sanctify the wine and transform its capacity for
evil into good, we also instill a measure of sanctity into
the weekdays and so transform their propensity for dulling
our spiritual aspirations into a propensity for increasing
our longing for God.

When we drink wine as part of the Havdalah ceremony,
in sanctifying the yield of the grape we distinguish good
from evil; we discriminate between authentic and spurious
spiritual experiences. In the process we purify the six
weekdays of the falsehood and evil that permeated them
when Adam ate from the Tree of Knowledge.

◆

HAVDALAH FRAGRANCE

Our souls derive sustenance from this world only through
the sense of smell. The fragrance of myrtle that we inhale
at the time of our Shabbat meals is thus meant to nourish

our souls. This altogether spiritual substance serves as the hors d'oeuvre for an entire meal of spiritual sustenance; it awakens within us the attentiveness we need to transform our eating into a conscious act of the mind and soul, whetting our appetites for the food's spiritual essence, not merely for the physical gratification it provides (see Section 2: "The Fragrance of Myrtles").

In the Havdalah ceremony at the end of Shabbat we nourish our souls once again with the fragrance of an aromatic herb or spice, to reinforce our souls one more time before partaking of any weekday food or drink. For unlike the meals of Shabbat, the meals we eat during the week are not inherently spiritual sustenance, nor do we generally eat those meals in the atmosphere of reflection and spiritual motivation that inheres at the Shabbat table. Thus, whereas the foods of Shabbat provide sustenance primarily for the brain, the seat of the soul, the foods we eat during the week provide sustenance primarily for the body.

Therefore, at the onset of a new week we again employ our sense of smell to nourish the brain and empower the soul. Our hope is that we can maintain, at least to some degree, the attentiveness of Shabbat; that we can extend this heightened awareness into our everyday consciousness and so focus throughout the week on the spiritual aspects of eating.

◆

HAVDALAH CANDLE

We kindle the Shabbat candles late Friday afternoon, somewhat before the day actually comes to a close, in order to draw the light of truth, which radiates in all its wholeness on Shabbat, into the half-truths of the weekdays. The healing embrace of this more perfect truth enables us to cultivate the responsiveness we need to see past the partial weekday-truths and summon the courage to take responsibility for every facet of our selves (see Section 2: "Candle Lighting").

As Shabbat departs, before the falling darkness can chase away the last traces of the holy day's radiance, we again kindle a light. We recite a blessing over this burning light as part of the *Havdalah* ceremony, with the same basic intent as we had when we kindled the candles on Friday afternoon: to illumine the partial truth of the weekdays with the wholeness of truth that radiates on Shabbat. Only by extending the pure truth of Shabbat into the darkness of the week can we hope to see our way through the illusion and obscurity of the weekdays, a mind-set that we set out to vanquish at the onset of Shabbat but that has now begun to resurface.

AN ILLUMINATION OF TIME

Shabbat is the foundation of the week; it is the center stem of a seven-branched candelabra. Like the menorah of the Holy Temple that stood in Jerusalem, each branch of this "candelabra of the week" is turned inward, facing the center; hence the fourth, fifth and sixth days of the week are illuminated by the spirit of the Shabbat to come; the first, second and third days are illuminated by the spirit of the Shabbat just passed. For Shabbat illuminates time, as it has done ever since the beginning of Creation.

(LIKUTEY HALAKHOT, ROSH CHODESH 7:55)

Eliyahu
the Prophet:
Unbound
By Time

On the night after Shabbat
it is customary to recite the verses
that mention the prophet Eliyahu and
to pray that he come and herald
the Redemption.

(Shulchan Arukh, Orach Chaim 295:1)

Eliyahu the prophet,
Eliyahu the Tishbite,
Eliyahu the Giladite—
May he come to us quickly,
ushering Mashaich, the son of David.

*B*ondage, in modern-day context, has yet to be abolished. Throughout the week we are bound to the material world and subjugated by its numerous demands and pressures. In short, we are slaves: slaves to our occupations and careers; slaves to our commitments and creditors; slaves to our need to provide for ourselves and for those who depend on us. Through asserting our control over the world—through stamping our mark on society—we are in fact enslaved: our bodies by our drive for achievement, our time by our race for success.

Jewish tradition teaches that the prophet Eliyahu will present himself at the time of the Final Redemption, to herald the arrival of Mashiach. Since the laws that prohibit travel on Shabbat prevent Mashiach from coming on the seventh day, the first possible time in the week when Eliyahu can come to announce the arrival of God's "anointed one" (*mashiach*) is on the night after Shabbat. It is for this reason that we praise Eliyahu's name in song at that time, calling on him to "come to us quickly, ushering Mashaich, the son of David."

The prophet Eliyahu personifies the awareness we hope to achieve when Shabbat is behind us and a new week begins. As Scripture relates, Eliyahu ascended to heaven alive. His perception of God had reached such an exalted plane that his soul did not need to separate from his body before ascending to a higher dimension. He entered the realm of "beyond-time" still garbed in his physical form.

Eliyahu is thus associated with the night that follows Shabbat. Through the relaxed atmosphere of Shabbat, we gain an inkling of what it is like to be beyond time; through refraining from the creative labor forbidden on the holy day, we enjoy a modicum of freedom from the bondage of materialism and corporeality. Now, with the week about to begin anew—as the weekday obligations, which we had set aside when Shabbat began, begin to reemerge and our workaday concerns are about to return—we would do well to employ this beyond-time consciousness to help us let go of the day-to-day concerns that rule our lives and impinge on our freedom.

In singing the praise of the prophet Eliyahu, we hope to draw inspiration from his example; as Eliyahu freed himself from the constrictions of time and matter, we dare hope that we, too, might liberate ourselves of the demands and pressures of the material world. And we pray that Eliyahu himself, as the harbinger of Redemption, might herald our personal redemption; that in the coming week we may experience spiritual, emotional, physical and practical freedom. ❁

TIME BEYOND TIME

Shabbat is a reminder of the World to Come; it is a taste, within time, of beyond-time.

Time was created through a delimiting of the infinite, as God constructed each new day through yet another abbreviation of eternity. During the week we, too, construct our days through delimiting our time, using contemporary tools such as day-planners and electronic schedulers.

But on Shabbat, the day's rites and rituals return us to the realm of the eternal, to time's origin, which is outside the construct of time. It is then that we get a taste of beyond-time…of time beyond in the World to Come.

◆

Fill the six weekdays with the beyond-time consciousness you obtain on Shabbat. Teach yourself to detach from the shackles of time and toil, to disengage from the worldly attachments you had believed you could not possibly live without.

(LIKUTEY HALAKHOT, MILAH 4:10, 13)

THE MELAVEH MALKA MEAL: INTO THE EVERYDAY

Even if one can eat only a small amount of food,
one should always set one's table
to escort the Shabbat as it departs.

(SHULCHAN ARUKH, ORACH CHAIM 300:1)

As with each of the three Shabbat meals,
it is the custom to begin the *Melaveh Malka* with
a salutation acknowledging the spiritual presence
in whose honor the meal is held.
Our guest at this fourth meal is King David;
the three Patriarchs, Avraham, Yitzchak and Yaakov,
join him.

Prepare the feast of perfect faith,
The joy of the Holy King.
Prepare the feast of the King.
This is the feast of David, the anointed king.
Avraham, Yitzchak and Yaakov
Come to feast with him.

Although Shabbat has departed, our Shabbat odyssey is not yet complete. We must carry the holiness of Shabbat into the weekdays and raise the everyday mentality of our lives with the higher awareness we gain on the seventh day.

With the appearance of the first stars on Saturday night, the Shabbat Queen, who has graced our homes and our spirits, departs. Unless we can return to the world of the marketplace armed with the heightened awareness of Shabbat, we will be hard-pressed to remain focused throughout the week on the subtler, spiritual aspects of life. Unless we can draw spirituality into the physical dimension, we will be hard-pressed to free ourselves of the enticements and demands of the material world, which begin to resurface with the inevitable reappearance of the weekdays.

For most of us, investing our day-to-day lives with higher levels of consciousness is a fierce battle. Inspiring our harried, workaday mind-set with Shabbat tranquility, transporting the seventh day's unique holiness into the mundanity of everyday reality, requires all the motivation, energy and skill we can muster.

No one was more effective at this than King David, the quintessential spiritual warrior. In all his battles, whether personal or military, David saw the deeper struggles of the spirit. His most dreaded foes were those who sought the destruction not of his body but of his soul. These were the primary forces that would undermine his spiritual standing, that would keep him from sanctifying the secular, from infusing the mundane with holiness—which is what David had in mind when he composed the psalms, pleading for God's salvation from the machinations of his enemies.

The Kabbalah teaches that David, king of Israel, is the personification of *Malkhut*, the *sefirah* (Divine emanation) through which God's Sovereignty is disseminated in the universe. *Malkhut's* function is to serve as the receptacle that brings the Light of the Divine Essence into the world of physical form.

Malkhut, which mediates between the earthly realm and the Divine, transmutes the Light into form, enabling it expression on earth. And while this is the purpose for which God created the Divine emanations, *Malkhut* in particular, worldly expression and transformation into earthly manifestation constitutes a descent into the realm of the physical, with all its attendant dangers. Hence David, as the embodiment of *Malkhut*, could be nothing less than the consummate spiritual warrior, for it was his task to transmit the light of heightened spiritual awareness into the everyday struggles of life.

The *Zohar* (I:248b) states:

> The Chariot of God consisted of three wheels—Avraham, Yitzchak and Yaakov. The Holy One then added King David as the fourth wheel, and the Divine Chariot was complete.

In the *Zohar's* metaphor, the Chariot symbolizes the vehicle through which God's Glory is "transported" from His hidden abode—His natural circumstance where He is absolutely unknowable and unconceivable—into the realm where He allows Himself to be visualized by those who are worthy. Because the three Patriarchs had made themselves into the vehicles for revealing God in the world, they came to personify the three "wheels" of His Chariot. Yet it was not until God included King David, as the fourth "wheel," that the vehicle for transporting the Light of the Divine Essence into this world was complete.

Each of the three Shabbat meals is associated with one of the Patriarchs, whose specific, outstanding qualities lend each meal its distinct ambiance. The compelling influence of Yitzchak graces the Friday night meal; he brings to it his traits of containment and receptivity and the introspective mode in which he relates to the world. The aura of Avraham surrounds the Shabbat morning meal; his trait of reaching out stirs the atmosphere with his active-expansive mode. Yaakov's energies enhance the Shabbat afternoon meal; he instills it with his quality of balance and the integrative mode through which can be discovered the oneness in all of life.

The fourth meal of Shabbat is *Melaveh Malka*, the meal we eat to escort the departing Shabbat Queen. *Melaveh Malka* is also the first meal of the new week. It is therefore fitting that this fourth meal is the feast of King David. Joined by Avraham, Yitzchak and Yaakov, David completes the Chariot that transports God to man, that transmits the holiness of Shabbat to the weekdays, that extends the higher awareness we gain on the seventh day into the everyday of our lives.

When we sit down to the fourth Shabbat meal, we recite a salutation acknowledging King David as the channel for drawing the spiritual into the physical dimension and as the spiritual presence in whose honor the meal of *Melaveh Malka* is held: *"Prepare the feast of perfect faith...This is the feast of David, the anointed king."* ⬤

1|א   SHABBAT: ON THE WAY IN (pages 8–53)

1.   *Likutey Moharan* I, 23; ibid. I, 86
2.   *Likutey Halakhot, Keriat HaTorah* 6:30
3.   *Likutey Moharan* I, 82; *Likutey Halakhot, Shechitah* 2:2
4.   *Likutey Halakhot, Geirim* 3:24
5.   *Likutey Halakhot, Betziat HaPat* 5:9,10
6.   *Likutey Moharan* II, 72; *Likutey Halakhot, Tefilin* 6:4
7.   *Nachat HaShulchan, Orach Chaim* #261
8.   *Likutey Halakhot, Shelichut veHarshaah* 4:14
9.   *Likutey Halakhot, Piryah veRivyah* 3:29; ibid. *Ishut* 4:33
10. *Likutey Halakhot, Kela'ey Beheimah* 4:4,5,7
11. *Likutey Halakhot, Piryah veRivyah* 3:29

2|ב   SHABBAT: THE NIGHT (pages 54–115)

1.   *Likutey Halakhot, Dayanim* 3:24
2.   *Likutey Halakhot, Maachaley Akum* 3:2,7
3.   *Likutey Halakhot, Eiruvey Techumin* 5:41
4.   *Likutey Halakhot, Umnin* 4:32
5.   *Likutey Halakhot, Kela'ey Beheimah* 4:11
6.   *Likutey Halakhot, Kela'ey Beheimah* 4:11; *Likutey Moharan* I, 79
7.   *Likutey Moharan* I, 52; *Yekara DeShabbata* I, 61
8.   *Likutey Halakhot, Shabbat* 6:1
9.   *Likutey Halakhot, Maachaley Akum* 2:1
10. *Likutey Halakhot, Milah* 4:10
11. *Likutey Halakhot, Betziat HaPat* 5:9
12. *Likutey Halakhot, Chakhirut veKablanut* 1:34
13. *Sichot HaRan* #155
14. *Likutey Halakhot, Eiruvey Techumin* 4:3
15. *Nachat HaShulchan, Orach Chaim* #261

GLOSSARY

Adam — human being

Amidah — the prayer of silent devotion, recited at each service

Atika Kadisha — "the Holy Ancient One"; the spiritual entity through which God's Supernal Will is manifest, corresponding to the Divine emanation of Keter (see below)

Binah — understanding

Chakal Tapuchin Kadishin — "the Sacred Orchard"; referring to the indwelling Presence of God (see Shekhinah), corresponding to the Divine emanation of Malkhut (see below)

Challah — special bread of Shabbat

Chokhmah — wisdom

Daat — knowledge

Dinim — "judgments"; agency of justice and punishment

Ein Sof — the Infinite One

Emunah — faith

Gan — garden

Haftarah — selection from a Book of Prophets read in synagogue Shabbat morning

Halakhah — the corpus of Jewish law

Havdalah — separation; ceremony concluding the Shabbat

Hitbodedut — secluded meditation and personal prayer to God

Kabbalah — receiving; the name of Judaism's mystical tradition

Kabbalat Shabbat — Friday evening prayer welcoming the Shabbat

Kavanah — focused concentration; intentionality

Kedushah — Sanctification Hymn recited in the Musaf prayer of Shabbat

Keter — the Divine emanation of God's "Crown"

Lechem Mishneh — two whole loaves of bread; "a double portion"

Maariv — the daily nighttime prayer

Malkhut — the Divine emanation through which God's Sovereignty is disseminated in the universe

Melakhah— creative labor; thirty-nine categories of "work" prohibited on Shabbat

Melaveh Malka— "fourth" meal of Shabbat

Menuchah— rest and repose; signifying a deep sense of tranquility and harmony

Mikvah — ritual purification bath

Minchah— the daily afternoon prayer

Mitzvah — commandment, of biblical or rabbinic origin

Musaf— additional prayer recited on Shabbat morning

Nahar— river

Neshamah Yeteirah— "added soul"; the extraordinary measure of holiness that Shabbat brings

Oneg— delight; a physical pleasure enjoyed on Shabbat

Rabbeinu— our teacher

Sefirah (pl. *Sefirot*) — any one of the ten Divine emanations that God created to direct the universe

Shacharit — the daily morning prayer

Shamor— "guard"; the commandment to be observe Shabbat

Shekhinah— indwelling Presence of God; the "feminine" aspect of the Divine

Sukkah— booth or tent

Targum— translation; Aramaic translation of the Torah

Tefillin— phylacteries

Teshuvah— repentance; an act of self-transformation and healing.

Tiferet— the Divine emanation of "Beauty"

Tikkun Olam— world-rectification; the world's social and spiritual transformation

Tzaddik (pl. *Tzaddikim*) — righteous individual

Tzimtzum— constriction; God's "contraction" of His Infinite Light.

Zachor— "remember"; the commandment to be mindful of Shabbat.

Zemirot — special table songs of Shabbat

Z'er Anpin— "the Lesser Countenance"; the spiritual entity through which Divine Providence is manifest, corresponding to the six Divine emanations encompassed in *Tiferet* (see above)

Zohar–the Book of Splendor, the basic text of Jewish mysticism

About the Breslov Research Institute

Rebbe Nachman was only 38 years old when he passed away in 1810. Yet, shortly before his passing, he told his followers that his influence would endure long afterwards. "My light will burn until the days of the Mashiach [Messiah]." Generations of readers have been enthralled and inspired by his writings, which have been explored and interpreted by leading scholars around the globe.

The growing interest in Rebbe Nachman from all sectors—academia and laymen alike—led to the establishment of the Breslov Research Institute in Jerusalem in 1979. Since then a team of scholars has been engaged in research into the texts, oral traditions and music of the Breslov movement. The purpose of the Institute is to publish authoritative translations, commentaries and general works on Breslov Chassidut. Projects also include the recording of Breslov songs and melodies on cassette and in music book form.

Offices and representatives of the Breslov Research Institute:

Israel:

Breslov Research Institute
P.O. Box 5370
Jerusalem, Israel
Tel: (011-9722) 582-4641
Fax: (011-9722) 582-5542
www.breslov.org

North America:

Breslov Research Institute
P.O. Box 587
Monsey, NY 10952-0587
Tel: (845) 425-4258
Fax: (845) 425-3018
www.breslov.org

Breslov books may be ordered directly from these offices or from Jewish Lights Publishing. Ordering information is provided at the end of this book.

BRESLOV RESEARCH INSTITUTE BOOKS

Rabbi Nachman's Stories
Translated by *Rabbi Aryeh Kaplan*
The Sages always told stories to convey some of the deepest secrets about God and His relation to the creation. Rebbe Nachman developed this ancient art to perfection. Spellbinding and entertaining, these stories are fast moving, richly structured and filled with penetrating insights. Rabbi Kaplan's translation is accompanied by a masterful commentary drawn from the works of Rebbe Nachman's chassidim.
6 x 9, 552 pages, HC, Bibliography, Index, ISBN 0-930213-02-5 **$21.00**

Crossing the Narrow Bridge
A Practical Guide to Rebbe Nachman's Teachings
by *Chaim Kramer;* ed. by *Moshe Mykoff*
Rebbe Nachman taught: "The world is a very narrow bridge. The main thing is not to be afraid." Lively, down to earth and easy to read, this book provides clear, detailed guidance in how to apply Rebbe Nachman's teachings in modern everyday life. Subjects include faith, joy, meditating, earning a living, health, raising children, etc., and provide a wealth of anecdotes from the lives of leading Breslov chassidim.
5½ x 8½, 452 pages, HC, Appendices, ISBN 0-930213-40-8 **$17.00**

The Breslov Haggadah
Compiled and translated by *Rabbi Yehoshua Starret* and *Chaim Kramer;* ed. by *Moshe Mykoff*
The classic Pesach Haggadah accompanied by Rebbe Nachman's unique insights and other commentary material drawn from Breslov and general sources. Includes appendices on: The Story of Exodus, Pesach Anecdotes, Chassidic insights into *Sefirat HaOmer, Chol HaMoed,* and *Shavuot.* 6½ x 9½, 256 pages, HC, Appendices, ISBN 0-930213-35-1 **$16.00**

Esther: *A Breslov Commentary on the Megillah*
Compiled and adapted by *Rabbi Yehoshua Starret*; ed. by *Ozer Bergman*
Insights from Rebbe Nachman and his followers that "unmask" the Megillah's deeper meaning in the modern context and for each of us personally. Includes Hebrew text of the Megillah, laws of the holiday and historical overview.
6 x 8½, 160 pages, PB, Appendices, ISBN 0-930213-42-4 **$12.00**

Chanukah—*With Rebbe Nachman of Breslov*
Compiled and adapted by *Rabbi Yehoshua Starret*
Traces the historical roots—and spiritual implications—of the Chanukah story, and provides deeper insight into the holiday's laws and their meaning for today. Based on the timeless wisdom of Rebbe Nachman and other Chassidic masters, this work lights the way on the journey from ancient Israel to the future, and into the mind and heart.
5 x 8, 128 pages, PB, ISBN 0-930213-99-8 **$10.00**

Garden of the Souls: *Rebbe Nachman on Suffering*
by *Avraham Greenbaum*
Offers guidance and comfort in dealing with pain and suffering in our own lives and those of the people around us. Faith makes it possible to find meaning in the trials of this world and turn them into experiences that can elevate us spiritually and open us to profound joy.
5 x 8, 96 pages, PB, ISBN 0-930213-39-4 **$8.00**

Anatomy of the Soul
by *Chaim Kramer*; ed. by *Avraham Sutton*
Explores the mystical meaning of the teaching that human beings are created in the image of God; provides an in-depth study of how the different systems of the human body relate to the ten *sefirot* and the five levels of the soul, and how through the body's organs and limbs we influence the hidden spiritual universes.
6 x 9, 364 pages, HC, Appendices, ISBN 0-930213-51-3 **$20.00**

Rabbi Nachman's Wisdom
Translated by *Rabbi Aryeh Kaplan*; ed. by *Rabbi Zvi Aryeh Rosenfeld*
A classic collection of Rebbe Nachman's conversations and teachings, ranging from comments on everyday practical topics to fundamental insights about faith and Jewish mysticism. The conversations provide a vivid picture of the Master, his wit, directness and wisdom. Also included is an account of Rebbe Nachman's adventure-filled pilgrimage to the Holy Land at the height of Napoleon's campaign in the Middle East in 1798.
6 x 9, 486 pages, HC, Appendices, Index, ISBN 0-930213-00-9 **$16.00**

Likutey Moharan: *The Collected Teachings of Rabbi Nachman*
Translated by *Moshe Mykoff*; annotated by *Chaim Kramer*
The first authoritative translation of Rebbe Nachman's *magnum opus*, presented with facing punctuated Hebrew text, full explanatory notes, source references and supplementary information relating to the lessons. Each volume is accompanied by appendices and charts clarifying pertinent kabbalistic concepts; the first volume includes Reb Noson's introduction to the original work, short biographies of leading Breslov personalities and a bibliography.

Vol. 1—*Lessons 1–6:* 6½ x 9½, HC, ISBN 0-930213-92-0 **$20.00**
Vol. 2—*Lessons 7–16:* 6½ x 9½, HC, ISBN 0-930213-93-9 **$20.00**
Vol. 3—*Lessons 17–22:* 6½ x 9½, HC, ISBN 0-930213-78-5 **$20.00**
Vol. 4—*Lessons 23–32:* 6½ x 9½, HC, ISBN 0-930213-79-3 **$20.00**
Vol. 5—*Lessons 33–48:* 6½ x 9½, HC, ISBN 0-930213-80-7 **$20.00**
Vol. 6—*Lessons 49–57:* 6½ x 9½, HC, ISBN 0-930213-81-5 **$20.00**
Vol. 7—*Lessons 58–64:* 6½ x 9½, HC, ISBN 0-930213-82-3 **$20.00**
Vol. 10—*Lessons 109–194:* 6½ x 9½, HC, ISBN 0-930213-85-8 **$20.00**
Vol. 11—*Lessons 195–286:* 6½ x 9½, HC, ISBN 0-930213-86-6 **$20.00**

Until the Mashiach

by *Rabbi Aryeh Kaplan*; ed. by *Rabbi Dovid Shapiro*

A scholarly research work that presents the events of Rebbe Nachman's life in a chronological format, with full source references throughout. Features an extensive historical overview, detailed maps and full appendices covering significant towns and cities, biographical information and anecdotes about Rebbe Nachman's family, pupils and other contemporary figures, his letters, a comprehensive family tree, and more.

6 x 9, 379 pages, HC, Appendices, Index, ISBN 0-930213-08-4 **$16.00**

Explorations: *A Mini-Series of Rebbe Nachman's Lessons*

Azamra—I Will Sing

Explores the way to happiness by finding the good in ourselves and in others.

4½ x 6½, 64 pages, PB, ISBN 0-930213-11-4 **$3.00**

Tsohar—Light

Explores the way through life's worst entanglement by shining the light of truth into all situations.

4½ x 6½, 64 pages, PB, ISBN 0-930213-26-2 **$3.00**

Mayim—Water

Explores free will based on the Talmudic teaching about the four who entered paradise.

4½ x 6½, 64 pages, PB, ISBN 0-930213-28-9 **$3.00**

Ayeh?—Where?

Explores how to find hope in even the darkest situations and turn them to one's advantage.

4½ x 6½, 64 pages, PB, ISBN 0-930213-12-2 **$3.00**

The Breslov Music Book: *Shabbat—Azamer Bishvochin (vol. 1)*

by *Ben-Zion Solomon*

The traditional music of the Breslov chassidim for Shabbat night prayers and meal, transcribed (with chords). Fully researched and annotated, includes history of each tune, vocalized Hebrew, facing English translation and transliteration.

8 x 11, 125 pages, PB, Spiral binding, ISBN 0-930213-36-X **$20.00**

The Breslov Music Book: *Shabbat—Asader LiS'udoso (vol. 2)*

by *Ben-Zion Solomon*

The traditional music of the Breslov chassidim for Shabbat morning prayers and the morning and afternoon meals, transcribed (with chords). Fully researched and annotated, includes history of each tune, vocalized Hebrew, facing English translation and transliteration. 8 x 11, 125 pages, PB, Spiral binding, ISBN 0-930213-60-2 **$20.00**

Audio Cassettes and CDs

Full-scale production of favorite Breslov Shabbat songs including some of Rebbe Nachman's own melodies. Cassettes **$12.00** each; CDs **$20.00** each.

Azamer Bishvochin—songs of the Shabbat evening prayers and the first meal

Me'eyn Olom Habo—songs of the first meal and the Shabbat morning prayers

Asader LiS'udoso—songs of the second Shabbat meal

B'nei Heicholo—songs of the third Shabbat meal

About JEWISH LIGHTS Publishing

People of all faiths and backgrounds yearn for books that attract, engage, educate, and spiritually inspire.

Our principal goal is to stimulate thought and help all people learn about who the Jewish People are, where they come from, and what the future can be made to hold. While people of our diverse Jewish heritage are the primary audience, our books speak to people in the Christian world as well and will broaden their understanding of Judaism and the roots of their own faith.

We bring to you authors who are at the forefront of spiritual thought and experience. While each has something different to say, they all say it in a voice that you can hear.

Our books are designed to welcome you and then to engage, stimulate, and inspire. We judge our success not only by whether or not our books are beautiful and commercially successful, but by whether or not they make a difference in your life.

We at Jewish Lights take great care to produce beautiful books that present meaningful spiritual content in a form that reflects the art of making high quality books. Therefore, we want to acknowledge those who contributed to the production of this book.

Stuart M. Matlins, Publisher

EDITORIAL
Lauren Seidman & Emily Wichland

COVER DESIGN & INTERIOR TYPESETTING
Tim Holtz

COVER / TEXT PRINTING & BINDING
Transcontinental Printing, Peterborough, Ontario

Life Cycle & Holidays

The Jewish Family Fun Book: *Holiday Projects, Everyday Activities, and Travel Ideas with Jewish Themes*
by *Danielle Dardashti* & *Roni Sarig*; Illustrated by *Avi Katz*

With almost 100 easy-to-do activities to re-invigorate age-old Jewish customs and make them fun for the whole family, this complete sourcebook details activities for fun at home and away from home, including meaningful everyday and holiday crafts, recipes, travel guides, enriching entertainment and much, much more. Illustrated.
6 x 9, 288 pp, Quality PB, Illus., ISBN 1-58023-171-3 **$18.95**

The Book of Jewish Sacred Practices
CLAL's Guide to Everyday & Holiday Rituals & Blessings
Ed. by *Rabbi Irwin Kula* & *Vanessa L. Ochs, Ph.D.*

A meditation, blessing, profound Jewish teaching, and ritual for more than one hundred everyday events and holidays. 6 x 9, 368 pp, Quality PB, ISBN 1-58023-152-7 **$18.95**

Celebrating Your New Jewish Daughter: *Creating Jewish Ways to Welcome Baby Girls into the Covenant—New and Traditional Ceremonies*
by Debra Nussbaum Cohen; Foreword by Sandy Eisenberg Sasso
6 x 9, 272 pp, Quality PB, ISBN 1-58023-090-3 **$18.95**

The New Jewish Baby Book AWARD WINNER!
Names, Ceremonies & Customs—A Guide for Today's Families
by Anita Diamant 6 x 9, 336 pp, Quality PB, ISBN 1-879045-28-1 **$18.95**

Parenting As a Spiritual Journey
Deepening Ordinary & Extraordinary Events into Sacred Occasions
by Nancy Fuchs-Kreimer 6 x 9, 224 pp, Quality PB, ISBN 1-58023-016-4 **$16.95**

Putting God on the Guest List, 2nd Ed. AWARD WINNER!
How to Reclaim the Spiritual Meaning of Your Child's Bar or Bat Mitzvah
by Rabbi Jeffrey K. Salkin 6 x 9, 224 pp, Quality PB, ISBN 1-879045-59-1 **$16.95**

The Bar/Bat Mitzvah Memory Book: *An Album for Treasuring the Spiritual Celebration* by Rabbi Jeffrey K. Salkin and Nina Salkin
8 x 10, 48 pp, Deluxe HC, 2-color text, ribbon marker, ISBN 1-58023-111-X **$19.95**

For Kids—Putting God on Your Guest List
How to Claim the Spiritual Meaning of Your Bar or Bat Mitzvah
by Rabbi Jeffrey K. Salkin 6 x 9, 144 pp, Quality PB, ISBN 1-58023-015-6 **$14.95**

Bar/Bat Mitzvah Basics, 2nd Ed.: *A Practical Family Guide to Coming of Age Together*
Ed. by Cantor Helen Leneman 6 x 9, 240 pp, Quality PB, ISBN 1-58023-151-9 **$18.95**

Hanukkah, 2nd Ed.: *The Family Guide to Spiritual Celebration*—The Art of Jewish Living
by Dr. Ron Wolfson 7 x 9, 240 pp, Quality PB, Illus., ISBN 1-58023-122-5 **$18.95**

Shabbat, 2nd Ed.: *Preparing for and Celebrating the Sabbath*—The Art of Jewish Living
by Dr. Ron Wolfson 7 x 9, 320 pp, Quality PB, Illus., ISBN 1-58023-164-0 **$19.95**

Passover, 2nd Ed.: *The Family Guide to Spiritual Celebration*—The Art of Jewish Living
by Dr. Ron Wolfson 7 x 9, 352 pp, Quality PB, ISBN 1-58023-174-8 **$19.95**

Children's Spirituality

Because Nothing Looks Like God

by *Lawrence and Karen Kushner*

Full-color illus. by *Dawn W. Majewski*

For ages 4 & up

MULTICULTURAL, NONDENOMINATIONAL, NONSECTARIAN

What is God like? The first collaborative work by husband-and-wife team Lawrence and Karen Kushner introduces children to the possibilities of spiritual life. Real-life examples of happiness and sadness—from goodnight stories, to the hope and fear felt the first time at bat, to the closing moments of life—invite us to explore, together with our children, the questions we all have about God, no matter what our age.

11 x 8½, 32 pp, HC, Full-color illus., ISBN 1-58023-092-X **$16.95**

*Also available: **Teacher's Guide,** 8½ x 11, 22 pp, PB, ISBN 1-58023-140-3 **$6.95** For ages 5–8*

Where Is God?
What Does God Look Like?
How Does God Make Things Happen? (Board Books)

For ages 0–4

by *Lawrence and Karen Kushner*; Full-color illus. by *Dawn W. Majewski*

Gently invites children to become aware of God's presence all around them. Three board books abridged from *Because Nothing Looks Like God* by Lawrence and Karen Kushner.

Each 5 x 5, 24 pp, Board, Full-color illus. **$7.95** SKYLIGHT PATHS Books

Sharing Blessings
Children's Stories for Exploring the Spirit of the Jewish Holidays

For ages 6 & up

by *Rahel Musleah* and *Rabbi Michael Klayman*; Full-color illus.

What is the spiritual message of each of the Jewish holidays? How do we teach it to our children? Through stories about one family's life, *Sharing Blessings* explores ways to get into the *spirit* of thirteen different holidays.

8½ x 11, 64 pp, HC, Full-color illus., ISBN 1-879045-71-0 **$18.95**

The Book of Miracles   AWARD WINNER!
A Young Person's Guide to Jewish Spiritual Awareness

For ages 9 & up

by *Lawrence Kushner*

Introduces kids to a way of everyday spiritual thinking to last a lifetime. Kushner, whose award-winning books have brought spirituality to life for countless adults, now shows young people how to use Judaism as a foundation on which to build their lives.

6 x 9, 96 pp, HC, 2-color illus., ISBN 1-879045-78-8 **$16.95**

Children's Spirituality

Cain & Abel   AWARD WINNER!
Finding the Fruits of Peace
by *Sandy Eisenberg Sasso*
Full-color illus. by *Joani Keller Rothenberg*

For ages 5 & up

A sensitive recasting of the ancient tale shows we have the power to deal with anger in positive ways. Provides questions for kids and adults to explore together. "Editor's Choice"—American Library Association's *Booklist*
9 x 12, 32 pp, HC, Full-color illus., ISBN 1-58023-123-3 **$16.95**

For Heaven's Sake   AWARD WINNER!
by *Sandy Eisenberg Sasso*; Full-color illus. by *Kathryn Kunz Finney*

For ages 4 & up

Everyone talked about heaven, but no one would say what heaven was or how to find it. So Isaiah decides to find out. 9 x 12, 32 pp, HC, Full-color illus., ISBN 1-58023-054-7 **$16.95**

God Said Amen   AWARD WINNER!
by *Sandy Eisenberg Sasso*; Full-color illus. by *Avi Katz*

For ages 4 & up

Inspiring tale of two kingdoms: one overflowing with water but without oil to light its lamps; the other blessed with oil but no water to grow its gardens. The kingdoms' rulers ask God for help but are too stubborn to ask each other. Shows that we need only reach out to each other to find God's answer to our prayers. 9 x 12, 32 pp, HC, Full-color illus., ISBN 1-58023-080-6 **$16.95**

God in Between   AWARD WINNER!
by *Sandy Eisenberg Sasso*; Full-color illus. by *Sally Sweetland*

For ages 4 & up

If you wanted to find God, where would you look? This magical, mythical tale teaches that God can be found where we are: within all of us and the relationships between us.
9 x 12, 32 pp, HC, Full-color illus., ISBN 1-879045-86-9 **$16.95**

Noah's Wife: *The Story of Naamah*
by *Sandy Eisenberg Sasso*; Full-color illus. by *Bethanne Andersen*   AWARD WINNER!

For ages 4 & up

Opens religious imaginations to new ideas about the story of the Flood. When God tells Noah to bring the animals onto the ark, God also calls on Naamah, Noah's wife, to save each plant on Earth. 9 x 12, 32 pp, HC, Full-color illus., ISBN 1-58023-134-9 **$16.95**

But God Remembered   AWARD WINNER!
Stories of Women from Creation to the Promised Land
by *Sandy Eisenberg Sasso*; Full-color illus. by *Bethanne Andersen*

For ages 8 & up

Vibrantly brings to life four stories of courageous and strong women from ancient tradition; all teach important values through their actions and faith.
9 x 12, 32 pp, HC, Full-color illus., ISBN 1-879045-43-5 **$16.95**

Healing/Wellness/Recovery

Jewish Paths toward Healing and Wholeness
A Personal Guide to Dealing with Suffering
by *Rabbi Kerry M. Olitzky*; Foreword by *Debbie Friedman*

Why me? Why do we suffer? How can we heal? Grounded in personal experience with illness and Jewish spiritual traditions, this book provides healing rituals, psalms and prayers that help readers initiate a dialogue with God, to guide them along the complicated path of healing and wholeness. 6 x 9, 192 pp, Quality PB, ISBN 1-58023-068-7 **$15.95**

Healing of Soul, Healing of Body
Spiritual Leaders Unfold the Strength & Solace in Psalms
Ed. by *Rabbi Simkha Y. Weintraub, CSW*, for The National Center for Jewish Healing

For those who are facing illness and those who care for them. Inspiring commentaries on ten psalms for healing by eminent spiritual leaders reflecting all Jewish movements make the power of the psalms accessible to all.
6 x 9, 128 pp, Quality PB, Illus., 2-color text, ISBN 1-879045-31-1 **$14.95**

Jewish Pastoral Care
A Practical Handbook from Traditional and Contemporary Sources
Ed. by *Rabbi Dayle A. Friedman*

Gives today's Jewish pastoral counselors practical guidelines based in the Jewish tradition.
6 x 9, 464 pp, HC, ISBN 1-58023-078-4 **$35.00**

Twelve Jewish Steps to Recovery: *A Personal Guide to Turning from Alcoholism & Other Addictions—Drugs, Food, Gambling, Sex . . .* by Rabbi Kerry M. Olitzky & Stuart A. Copans, M.D. Preface by Abraham J. Twerski, M.D.; "Getting Help" by JACS Foundation 6 x 9, 144 pp, Quality PB, ISBN 1-879045-09-5 **$14.95**

One Hundred Blessings Every Day: *Daily Twelve Step Recovery Affirmations, Exercises for Personal Growth & Renewal Reflecting Seasons of the Jewish Year* by Rabbi Kerry M. Olitzky 4½ x 6½, 432 pp, Quality PB, ISBN 1-879045-30-3 **$14.95**

Recovery from Codependence: *A Jewish Twelve Steps Guide to Healing Your Soul* by Rabbi Kerry M. Olitzky 6 x 9, 160 pp, Quality PB, ISBN 1-879045-32-X **$13.95**

Renewed Each Day: *Daily Twelve Step Recovery Meditations Based on the Bible* by Rabbi Kerry M. Olitzky & Aaron Z. *Vol. I: Genesis & Exodus; Vol. II: Leviticus, Numbers and Deuteronomy*
Vol. I: 6 x 9, 224 pp, Quality PB, ISBN 1-879045-12-5 **$14.95**
Vol. II: 6 x 9, 280 pp, Quality PB, ISBN 1-879045-13-3 **$14.95**

Theology/Philosophy

Ehyeh: *A Kabbalah for Tomorrow*
by *Arthur Green*

Distills a forty-year search for wisdom by one of the world's leading interpreters of the Jewish mystical tradition who shares the fundamental ideas and spiritual teachings of Kabbalah. Explains how the ancient language of Kabbalah can be retooled to address the needs of our generation. 6 x 9, 224 pp, HC, ISBN 1-58023-125-X **$21.95**

Love and Terror in the God Encounter
The Theological Legacy of Rabbi Joseph B. Soloveitchik
by *Dr. David Hartman*

Renowned scholar David Hartman explores the sometimes surprising intersection of Soloveitchik's rootedness in halakhic tradition with his genuine responsiveness to modern Western theology. An engaging look at one of the most important Jewish thinkers of the twentieth century.
6 x 9, 240 pp, Quality PB, ISBN 1-58023-176-4 **$19.95**; HC, ISBN 1-58023-112-8 **$25.00**

These Are the Words: *A Vocabulary of Jewish Spiritual Life*
by *Arthur Green*

What are the most essential ideas, concepts and terms that an educated person needs to know about Judaism? From *Adonai* (My Lord) to *zekhut* (merit), this enlightening and entertaining journey through Judaism teaches us the 149 core Hebrew words that constitute the basic vocabulary of Jewish spiritual life. 6 x 9, 304 pp, Quality PB, ISBN 1-58023-107-1 **$18.95**

    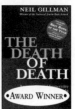

Broken Tablets: *Restoring the Ten Commandments and Ourselves* AWARD WINNER!
Ed. by Rachel S. Mikva; Intro. by Lawrence Kushner
6 x 9, 192 pp, Quality PB, ISBN 1-58023-158-6 **$16.95**; HC, ISBN 1-58023-066-0 **$21.95**

A Heart of Many Rooms: *Celebrating the Many Voices within Judaism* AWARD WINNER!
by Dr. David Hartman 6 x 9, 352 pp, Quality PB, ISBN 1-58023-156-X **$19.95**;
HC, ISBN 1-58023-048-2 **$24.95**

A Living Covenant: *The Innovative Spirit in Traditional Judaism* AWARD WINNER!
by Dr. David Hartman 6 x 9, 368 pp, Quality PB, ISBN 1-58023-011-3 **$18.95**

The Death of Death: *Resurrection and Immortality in Jewish Thought* AWARD WINNER!
by Dr. Neil Gillman 6 x 9, 336 pp, Quality PB, ISBN 1-58023-081-4 **$18.95**

The Last Trial: *On the Legends and Lore of the Command to Abraham to Offer Isaac as a Sacrifice* by Shalom Spiegel 6 x 9, 208 pp, Quality PB, ISBN 1-879045-29-X **$17.95**

Tormented Master: *The Life and Spiritual Quest of Rabbi Nahman of Bratslav*
by Dr. Arthur Green 6 x 9, 416 pp, Quality PB, ISBN 1-879045-11-7 **$18.95**

The Earth Is the Lord's: *The Inner World of the Jew in Eastern Europe*
by Abraham Joshua Heschel 5½ x 8, 128 pp, Quality PB, ISBN 1-879045-42-7 **$14.95**

A Passion for Truth: *Despair and Hope in Hasidism* by Abraham Joshua Heschel
5½ x 8, 352 pp, Quality PB, ISBN 1-879045-41-9 **$18.95**

Your Word Is Fire: *The Hasidic Masters on Contemplative Prayer* Ed. by Dr. Arthur Green and Dr. Barry W. Holtz 6 x 9, 160 pp, Quality PB, ISBN 1-879045-25-7 **$15.95**

Spirituality—The Kushner Series
Books by Lawrence Kushner

The Way Into Jewish Mystical Tradition
Explains the principles of Jewish mystical thinking, their religious and spiritual significance, and how they relate to our lives. A book that allows us to experience and understand the Jewish mystical approach to our place in the world.
6 x 9, 224 pp, HC, ISBN 1-58023-029-6 **$21.95**

Jewish Spirituality: *A Brief Introduction for Christians*
Addresses Christian's questions, revealing the essence of Judaism in a way that people whose own tradition traces its roots to Judaism can understand and appreciate.
5½ x 8½, 112 pp, Quality PB, ISBN 1-58023-150-0 **$12.95**

Eyes Remade for Wonder: *The Way of Jewish Mysticism and Sacred Living*
A Lawrence Kushner Reader Intro. by *Thomas Moore*

Whether you are new to Kushner or a devoted fan, you'll find inspiration here. With samplings from each of Kushner's works, and a generous amount of new material, this book is to be read and reread, each time discovering deeper layers of meaning in our lives.
6 x 9, 240 pp, Quality PB, ISBN 1-58023-042-3 **$18.95**; HC, ISBN 1-58023-014-8 **$23.95**

   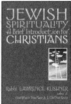 

Invisible Lines of Connection: *Sacred Stories of the Ordinary* AWARD WINNER!
5½ x 8½, 160 pp, Quality PB, ISBN 1-879045-98-2 **$15.95**

Honey from the Rock: *An Introduction to Jewish Mysticism* SPECIAL ANNIVERSARY EDITION
6 x 9, 176 pp, Quality PB, ISBN 1-58023-073-3 **$15.95**

The Book of Letters: *A Mystical Hebrew Alphabet* AWARD WINNER!
Popular HC Edition, 6 x 9, 80 pp, 2-color text, ISBN 1-879045-00-1 **$24.95**; *Deluxe Gift Edition*, 9 x 12, 80 pp, HC, 4-color text, ornamentation, slipcase, ISBN 1-879045-01-X **$79.95**; *Collector's Limited Edition*, 9 x 12, 80 pp, HC, gold-embossed pages, hand-assembled slipcase. With silkscreened print. Limited to 500 signed and numbered copies, ISBN 1-879045-04-4 **$349.00**

The Book of Words: *Talking Spiritual Life, Living Spiritual Talk* AWARD WINNER!
6 x 9, 160 pp, Quality PB, 2-color text, ISBN 1-58023-020-2 **$16.95**; HC, ISBN 1-879045-35-4 **$21.95**

God Was in This Place & I, i Did Not Know: *Finding Self, Spirituality and Ultimate Meaning*
6 x 9, 192 pp, Quality PB, ISBN 1-879045-33-8 **$16.95**

The River of Light: *Jewish Mystical Awareness* SPECIAL ANNIVERSARY EDITION
6 x 9, 192 pp, Quality PB, ISBN 1-58023-096-2 **$16.95**

Because Nothing Looks Like God
by Lawrence and Karen Kushner; Full-color illus. by Dawn W. Majewski
11 x 8½, 32 pp, HC, Full-color illus., ISBN 1-58023-092-X **$16.95** **For ages 4 & up**

Spirituality & More

The Jewish Lights Spirituality Handbook
A Guide to Understanding, Exploring & Living a Spiritual Life
Ed. by *Stuart M. Matlins, Editor in Chief, Jewish Lights Publishing*

Rich, creative material from over fifty spiritual leaders on every aspect of Jewish spirituality today: prayer, meditation, mysticism, study, rituals, special days, the everyday, and more. For all ages.
6 x 9, 456 pp, Quality PB, ISBN 1-58023-093-8 **$18.95**; HC, ISBN 1-58023-100-4 **$24.95**

The Story of the Jews: *A 4,000-Year Adventure—A Graphic History Book*
Written and illustrated by *Stan Mack*

Through witty cartoons and accurate narrative, illustrates the major characters and events that have shaped the Jewish people and culture. For all ages.
6 x 9, 304 pp, Quality PB, Illus., ISBN 1-58023-155-1 **$16.95**

The Jewish Prophet: *Visionary Words from Moses and Miriam to Henrietta Szold and A. J. Heschel*
by *Rabbi Dr. Michael J. Shire*

This beautifully illustrated collection of Jewish prophecy features the lives and teachings of thirty men and women, from biblical times to modern day. Provides an inspiring and informative description of the role each played in their own time, and an explanation of why we should know about them in our time. Illustrated with illuminations from medieval Hebrew manuscripts.
6½ x 8½, 128 pp, HC, 123 full-color illus., ISBN 1-58023-168-3 **$25.00**

The Enneagram and Kabbalah: *Reading Your Soul*
by Rabbi Howard A. Addison 6 x 9, 176 pp, Quality PB, ISBN 1-58023-001-6 **$15.95**

Cast in God's Image: *Discover Your Personality Type Using the Enneagram and Kabbalah*
by Rabbi Howard A. Addison 7 x 9, 176 pp, Quality PB, ISBN 1-58023-124-1 **$16.95**

Mystery Midrash: *An Anthology of Jewish Mystery & Detective Fiction* AWARD WINNER!
Ed. by Lawrence W. Raphael 6 x 9, 304 pp, Quality PB, ISBN 1-58023-055-5 **$16.95**

Criminal Kabbalah: *An Intriguing Anthology of Jewish Mystery & Detective Fiction*
Ed. by Lawrence W. Raphael; Foreword by Laurie R. King
6 x 9, 256 pp, Quality PB, ISBN 1-58023-109-8 **$16.95**

Sacred Intentions: *Daily Inspiration to Strengthen the Spirit, Based on Jewish Wisdom*
by Rabbis Kerry M. Olitzky & Lori Forman
4½ x 6½, 448 pp, Quality PB, ISBN 1-58023-061-X **$16.95**

Restful Reflections: *Nighttime Inspiration to Calm the Soul, Based on Jewish Wisdom*
by Rabbis Kerry M. Olitzky & Lori Forman
4½ x 6½, 448 pp, Quality PB, ISBN 1-58023-091-1 **$15.95**

Embracing the Covenant: *Converts to Judaism Talk About Why & How* Ed. by Rabbi Allan Berkowitz & Patti Moskovitz 6 x 9, 192 pp, Quality PB, ISBN 1-879045-50-8 **$16.95**

Wandering Stars: *An Anthology of Jewish Fantasy & Science Fiction* Ed. by Jack Dann; Intro. by Isaac Asimov 6 x 9, 272 pp, Quality PB, ISBN 1-58023-005-9 **$16.95**

Israel—A Spiritual Travel Guide: *A Companion for the Modern Jewish Pilgrim* AWARD WINNER!
by Rabbi Lawrence A. Hoffman 4¼ x 10, 256 pp, Quality PB, ISBN 1-879045-56-7 **$18.95**

Jewish Meditation

Aleph-Bet Yoga
Embodying the Hebrew Letters for Physical and Spiritual Well-Being
by *Steven A. Rapp*; Foreword by *Tamar Frankiel* & *Judy Greenfeld*; Preface by *Hart Lazer*

Blends aspects of hatha yoga and the shapes of the Hebrew letters. Connects yoga practice with Jewish spiritual life. Easy-to-follow instructions, b/w photos.
7 x 10, 128 pp, Quality PB, b/w photos, ISBN 1-58023-162-4 **$16.95**

The Rituals & Practices of a Jewish Life
A Handbook for Personal Spiritual Renewal
by *Rabbi Kerry M. Olitzky* and *Rabbi Daniel Judson*; Foreword by *Vanessa L. Ochs*; Illustrated by *Joel Moskowitz*

This easy-to-use handbook explains the why, what, and how of ten specific areas of Jewish ritual and practice: morning and evening blessings, covering the head, blessings throughout the day, daily prayer, tefillin, tallit and *tallit katan*, Torah study, kashrut, *mikvah*, and entering Shabbat. 6 x 9, 272 pp, Quality PB, Illus., ISBN 1-58023-169-1 **$18.95**

Discovering Jewish Meditation: *Instruction & Guidance for Learning an Ancient Spiritual Practice* by Nan Fink Gefen 6 x 9, 208 pp, Quality PB, ISBN 1-58023-067-9 **$16.95**

The Handbook of Jewish Meditation Practices: *A Guide for Enriching the Sabbath and Other Days of Your Life* by Rabbi David A. Cooper
6 x 9, 208 pp, Quality PB, ISBN 1-58023-102-0 **$16.95**

Meditation from the Heart of Judaism: *Today's Teachers Share Their Practices, Techniques, and Faith* Ed. by Avram Davis 6 x 9, 256 pp, Quality PB, ISBN 1-58023-049-0 **$16.95**

The Way of Flame: *A Guide to the Forgotten Mystical Tradition of Jewish Meditation* by Avram Davis 4½ x 8, 176 pp, Quality PB, ISBN 1-58023-060-1 **$15.95**

Minding the Temple of the Soul: *Balancing Body, Mind, and Spirit through Traditional Jewish Prayer, Movement, and Meditation* by Tamar Frankiel and Judy Greenfeld
7 x 10, 184 pp, Quality PB, Illus., ISBN 1-879045-64-8 **$16.95**

Entering the Temple of Dreams: *Jewish Prayers, Movements, and Meditations for the End of the Day* by Tamar Frankiel and Judy Greenfeld
7 x 10, 192 pp, Illus., Quality PB, ISBN 1-58023-079-2 **$16.95**

 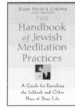   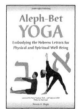

Ecology

Torah of the Earth: Exploring 4,000 Years of Ecology in Jewish Thought
In 2 Volumes Ed. by *Rabbi Arthur Waskow*

An invaluable key to understanding the intersection of ecology and Judaism. Leading scholars provide a guided tour of Jewish ecological thought.
Vol. 1: *Biblical Israel & Rabbinic Judaism*, 6 x 9, 272 pp, Quality PB, ISBN 1-58023-086-5 **$19.95**
Vol. 2: *Zionism & Eco-Judaism*, 6 x 9, 336 pp, Quality PB, ISBN 1-58023-087-3 **$19.95**

Ecology & the Jewish Spirit: *Where Nature & the Sacred Meet* Ed. and with Intros.
by Ellen Bernstein 6 x 9, 288 pp, Quality PB, ISBN 1-58023-082-2 **$16.95**

Spirituality

My People's Prayer Book: *Traditional Prayers, Modern Commentaries*
Ed. by *Dr. Lawrence A. Hoffman*

Provides a diverse and exciting commentary to the traditional liturgy, helping modern men and women find new wisdom in Jewish prayer, and bring liturgy into their lives. Each book includes Hebrew text, modern translation, and commentaries *from all perspectives* of the Jewish world.

Vol. 1—*The Sh'ma and Its Blessings*, 7 x 10, 168 pp, HC, ISBN 1-879045-79-6 **$23.95**
Vol. 2—*The Amidah*, 7 x 10, 240 pp, HC, ISBN 1-879045-80-X **$24.95**
Vol. 3—*P'sukei D'zimrah* (Morning Psalms), 7 x 10, 240 pp, HC, ISBN 1-879045-81-8 **$24.95**
Vol. 4—*Seder K'riat Hatorah* (The Torah Service), 7 x 10, 264 pp, HC, ISBN 1-879045-82-6 **$23.95**
Vol. 5—*Birkhot Hashachar* (Morning Blessings), 7 x 10, 240 pp, HC, ISBN 1-879045-83-4 **$24.95**
Vol. 6—*Tachanun and Concluding Prayers*, 7 x 10, 240 pp, HC, ISBN 1-879045-84-2 **$24.95**

Six Jewish Spiritual Paths: *A Rationalist Looks at Spirituality*
by Rabbi Rifat Sonsino
6 x 9, 208 pp, Quality PB, ISBN 1-58023-167-5 **$16.95**; HC, ISBN 1-58023-095-4 **$21.95**

Becoming a Congregation of Learners
Learning as a Key to Revitalizing Congregational Life by Isa Aron, Ph.D.;
Foreword by Rabbi Lawrence A. Hoffman, Co-Developer, Synagogue 2000
6 x 9, 304 pp, Quality PB, ISBN 1-58023-089-X **$19.95**

Self, Struggle & Change
Family Conflict Stories in Genesis and Their Healing Insights for Our Lives
by Dr. Norman J. Cohen 6 x 9, 224 pp, Quality PB, ISBN 1-879045-66-4 **$16.95**

Voices from Genesis: *Guiding Us through the Stages of Life*
by Dr. Norman J. Cohen 6 x 9, 192 pp, Quality PB, ISBN 1-58023-118-7 **$16.95**

Ancient Secrets: *Using the Stories of the Bible to Improve Our Everyday Lives*
by Rabbi Levi Meier, Ph.D. 5½ x 8½, 288 pp, Quality PB, ISBN 1-58023-064-4 **$16.95**

The Business Bible: *10 New Commandments for Bringing Spirituality & Ethical Values into the Workplace*
by Rabbi Wayne Dosick 5½ x 8½, 208 pp, Quality PB, ISBN 1-58023-101-2 **$14.95**

Being God's Partner: *How to Find the Hidden Link Between Spirituality and Your Work*
by Rabbi Jeffrey K. Salkin; Intro. by Norman Lear **AWARD WINNER!**
6 x 9, 192 pp, Quality PB, ISBN 1-879045-65-6 **$17.95**; HC, ISBN 1-879045-37-0 **$19.95**

God & the Big Bang
Discovering Harmony Between Science & Spirituality **AWARD WINNER!**
by Daniel C. Matt 6 x 9, 224 pp, Quality PB, ISBN 1-879045-89-3 **$16.95**

Soul Judaism: *Dancing with God into a New Era*
by Rabbi Wayne Dosick 5½ x 8½, 304 pp, Quality PB, ISBN 1-58023-053-9 **$16.95**

Finding Joy: *A Practical Spiritual Guide to Happiness* **AWARD WINNER!**
by Rabbi Dannel I. Schwartz with Mark Hass
6 x 9, 192 pp, Quality PB, ISBN 1-58023-009-1 **$14.95**; HC, ISBN 1-879045-53-2 **$19.95**

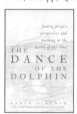